PISCES
WITCH

♓

©JAMES C. WELCH

Ivo Dominguez, Jr. (Georgetown, DE) has been active in the magickal community since 1978. He is one of the founders of Keepers of the Holly Chalice, the first Assembly of the Sacred Wheel coven. He currently serves as one of the Elders in the Assembly. Ivo is the author of several books, including *The Four Elements of the Wise* and *Practical Astrology for Witches and Pagans*. In his mundane life, he has been a computer programmer, the executive director of an AIDS/HIV service organization, a bookstore owner, and many other things. Visit him at www.ivodominguezjr.com.

© SHANE ERNEST

Mat Auryn is an acclaimed author of award-winning bestselling books such as *Psychic Witch* and *Mastering Magick*. He is a Pisces witch, teacher, speaker, and retired psychic, with decades of experience and initiation into various witchcraft traditions and esoteric orders. He teaches at Modern Witch University, writes for various publications including *Witches & Pagans Magazine*, and his work is displayed at the Buckland Museum of Witchcraft and Magick. Mat is also co-owner of Datura Trading, Co. More at Auryn.net or on Instagram @MatAuryn.

UNLOCK THE MAGIC OF YOUR SUN SIGN

PISCES
WITCH

IVO DOMINGUEZ, JR.
MAT AURYN

Llewellyn Publications
Woodbury, Minnesota

FIRST EDITION
First Printing, 2024

Art direction and cover design by Shira Atakpu
Book design by Christine Ha
Interior art by the Llewellyn Art Department
Neptunian Eye Sigil by Mat Auryn
Tarot Original 1909 Deck © 2021 with art created by Pamela Colman Smith and Arthur Edward Waite. Used with permission of LoScarabeo.
The Pisces Correspondences appendix is excerpted with permission from *Llewellyn's Complete Book of Correspondences: A Comprehensive & Cross-Referenced Resource for Pagans & Wiccans* © 2013 by Sandra Kynes.

Llewellyn Publications is a registered trademark of Llewellyn Worldwide Ltd.

Library of Congress Cataloging-in-Publication Data
Names: Domínguez, Ivo, Jr., author. | Auryn, Mat, author.
Title: Pisces witch : unlock the magic of your sun sign : swimming the
  starry seas / Ivo Dominguez, Jr. and Mat Auryn.
Description: First edition. | Woodbury, MN : Llewellyn Publications, [2024]
  | Series: The witch's sun sign series ; 12
Identifiers: LCCN 2024015008 (print) | LCCN 2024015009 (ebook) | ISBN
  9780738772912 (paperback) | ISBN 9780738772974 (ebook)
Subjects: LCSH: Pisces (Astrology) | Witchcraft. | Magic.
Classification: LCC BF1727.75 .D66 2024 (print) | LCC BF1727.75 (ebook) |
  DDC 133.5/277—dc23/eng/20240509
LC record available at https://lccn.loc.gov/2024015008
LC ebook record available at https://lccn.loc.gov/2024015009

Llewellyn Worldwide Ltd. does not participate in, endorse, or have any authority or responsibility concerning private business transactions between our authors and the public.

All mail addressed to the author is forwarded but the publisher cannot, unless specifically instructed by the author, give out an address or phone number.

Any internet references contained in this work are current at publication time, but the publisher cannot guarantee that a specific location will continue to be maintained. Please refer to the publisher's website for links to authors' websites and other sources.

Llewellyn Publications
A Division of Llewellyn Worldwide Ltd.
2143 Woodedale Drive
Woodbury, MN 55125-2989
www.llewellyn.com

Printed in the United States of America

CONTENTS

Contents

SPELLS, RECIPES, AND PRACTICES

INTRODUCTION

Ivo Dominguez, Jr.

This is the twelfth and last book in the Witch's Sun Sign series. There are twelve volumes in this series with a book for every Sun sign, but with a special focus on witchcraft. This series explores and honors the gifts, perspectives, and joys of being a witch through the perspective of their Sun sign. Each book has information on how your sign affects your magick and life experiences with insights provided by witches of your Sun sign, as well as spells, rituals, and practices to enrich your witchcraft. This series is geared toward helping witches grow, develop, and integrate the power of their Sun sign into all their practices. Each book in the series has ten writers, so there are many takes on the meaning of being a witch of a particular sign. All the books in the Witch's Sun Sign series are a sampler of possibilities, with pieces that are deep, fun, practical, healing, instructive, revealing, and authentic.

Welcome to the Pisces Witch

I'm Ivo Dominguez, Jr., and I've been a witch and an astrologer for over forty years. In this book, and in the whole series, I've written the chapters focused on astrological information and collaborated with the other writers. For the sake of transparency, I am a Sagittarius, and the majority of the other writers for this book are Pisces.[1] The chapters focused on the lived experiences of being a Pisces witch were written by my coauthor, Mat Auryn, who is a teacher, psychic, multi-award-winning author, tarot reader, and High Priest in the Sacred Fires Tradition of Witchcraft. The spells and shorter pieces written for this book come from a diverse group of strong Pisces witches. Their practices will give you a deeper understanding of yourself as a Pisces and as a witch. With the information, insights, and methods offered here, your Pisces nature and your witchcraft will be better united. The work of becoming fully yourself entails finding, refining, and merging all the parts that make up your life and identity. This all sounds very serious, but the content of this book will run from lighthearted to profound to do justice to the topic. Moreover, this book has practical suggestions on using the power of your Sun sign to improve your craft as a witch. There are many books on Pisces or

---

1. The exceptions are Dawn Aurora Hunt, who contributes a recipe for each sign in the series, and Sandra Kynes, whose correspondences are listed in the appendix.

astrology or witchcraft; this book is about wholeheartedly being a Pisces witch.

There is a vast amount of material available in books, blogs, memes, and videos targeted at Pisces. The content presented in these ranges from serious to snarky, and a fair amount of it is less than accurate or useful. After reading this book, you will be better equipped to tell which of these you can take to heart and use, and which are fine for a laugh but not much more. There is a good chance you will be flipping back to reread some chapters to get a better understanding of some of the points being made. This book is meant to be read more than once, and some parts of it may become reference material you will use for years. Consider keeping a folder, digital or paper, for your notes and ideas on being a Pisces witch.

What You Will Need

Knowing your Sun sign is enough to get quite a bit out of this book. However, to use all the material in this book, you will need your birth chart to verify your Moon sign and rising sign. In addition to your birth date, you will need the location and the time of your birth as exactly as possible. If you don't know your birth time, try to get a copy of your birth certificate (though not all birth certificates list times). If it is reasonable and you feel comfortable, you can ask family members for information. They may remember an exact time, but even narrowing it down to a range of hours will be useful.

There is a solution to not having your exact birth time. Since it takes moments to create birth charts using software, you can run birth charts that are thirty minutes apart over the span of hours that contain your possible birth times. By reading the chapters that describe the characteristics of Moon signs and rising signs, you can reduce the pile of possible charts to a few contenders. Read the descriptions and find the chart whose combination of Moon sign and rising sign rings true to you.

There are more refined techniques a professional astrologer can use to get closer to a chart that is more accurate. However, knowing your Sun sign, Moon sign, and rising is all you need for this book. There are numerous websites that offer free basic birth charts you can view online. For a fee, more detailed charts are available on these sites.

You may want to have an astrological wall calendar or an astrological day planner to keep track of the sign and phase of the Moon. You will want to keep track of what your ruling planet, Neptune, is doing. Over time as your knowledge grows, you'll probably start looking at where all the planets are, what aspects they are making, and when they are retrograde or direct. You could do this all on an app or a website, but it is often easier to flip through a calendar or planner to see what is going on. Flipping forward and back through the weeks and months ahead can give you a better sense of how to prepare for upcoming celestial influences. Moreover, the calendars and planner contain basic background information about astrology and are a great start for studying astrology.

You're a Pisces and So Much More

Every person is unique, complex, and a mixture of traits that can clash, complement, compete, or collaborate with each other. This book focuses on your Pisces Sun sign and provides starting points for understanding your Moon sign and rising sign. It cannot answer all your questions or be a perfect fit because of all the other parts that make you an individual. However, you will find more than enough to enrich and deepen your witchcraft as a Pisces. There will also be descriptions you won't agree with or that you think do not portray you. In some instances, you will be correct, and in other cases, you may come around to acknowledging that the information does apply to you. Astrology can be used for magick, divination, personal development, and more. No matter the purpose, your understanding of astrology will change over time as your life unfolds and your experience and self-knowledge broaden. You will probably return to this book several times as you find opportunities to use more of the insights and methods.

This may seem like strange advice to find in a book for the Pisces witch, but remember that you are more than a Pisces witch. In the process of claiming the identity of being a witch, it is common to want to have a clear and firm definition of

5

who you are. Sometimes this means overidentifying with a category, such as water witch, herb witch, crystal witch, kitchen witch, and so on. It is useful to become aware of the affinities you have so long as you do not limit and bind yourself to being less than you are. The best use for this book is to uncover all the Pisces parts of you so you can integrate them well. The finest witches I know have well-developed specialties, but also are well rounded in their knowledge and practices.

Onward!

With all that said, the Sun is the starting point for your power and your journey as a witch. The first chapter is about the profound influence your Sun sign has, so don't skip through the table of contents; please start at the beginning. After that, Mat will dive into magick and practices that come naturally to Pisces witches. I'll be walking you through the benefits of picking the right times, places, and things to energize your Pisces magick. Mat will also share a couple of real-life personal stories on his ups and downs, as well as advice on the best ways to protect yourself spiritually and set good boundaries when you really need to. I'll introduce you to how your Moon sign and your rising sign shape your witchcraft. Mat offers great stories about how his Pisces nature comes forward in his life as a witch, and then gives suggestions on self-care and self-awareness. I'll share a full ritual with you to call on the spirit of your sign. Lastly, Mat offers his wisdom on how to become a better Pisces witch. Throughout the whole book, you'll find tables of correspondences, spells, recipes, techniques, and other treasures to add to your practices.

HOW YOUR SUN
POWERS YOUR MAGICK

Ivo Dominguez, Jr.

The first bit of astrology that people generally learn is their Sun sign. Some enthusiastically embrace the meaning of their Sun sign and apply it to everything in their life. They feel their Sun is shining and all is well in the world. Then at some point they'll encounter someone who will, with a bit of disdain, enlighten them on the limits of Sun sign astrology. They feel their Sun isn't enough and they scramble to catch up. What comes next is usually the discovery that they have a Moon sign, a rising sign, and all the rest of the planets in an assortment of signs. Making sense of all this additional information is daunting as it requires quite a bit of learning and/or an astrologer to guide you through the process. Wherever you are in this or similar journeys into the world of astrology, at some point you will circle back around and rediscover that the Sun is still in the center.

The Sun in your birth chart shows where life and spirit came into the world to form you. It is the keeper of your spark of spirit and the wellspring of your power. Your Sun is in Pisces, so that is the flavor, the color, the type of energy that is at your core. You are your whole birth chart, but it is your Pisces Sun that provides the vital force that moves throughout all parts of your life. When you work in harmony and alignment with your Sun, you have access to more life and the capacity to live it better. This is true for all people, but this advice takes on a special meaning for those who are witches. The root of a witch's magick power is revealed by their Sun sign. You can draw on many kinds of energy, but the type of energy that you attract with greatest ease is Pisces. The more awareness and intention you apply to connecting with and acting as a conduit for that Pisces Sun, the more effective you will be as a witch.

The more you learn about the meaning of a Pisces Sun, the easier it will be to find ways to make that connection. To be effective in magick, divination, and other categories of workings, it is vital that you understand yourself—your motivations, drives, attractions, and so on—so that you can refine your intentions, questions, and desired outcomes. Understanding your Pisces sign is an important step in that process. One of the goals shared by both witchcraft and astrology is to affirm and to integrate the totality of your nature to live your best life. The glyph for the Sun in astrology is a dot with

a circle around it. Your Pisces Sun is the dot and
the circle, your center, and your circumference. It is
your beginning and your journey. It is also the core
of your personal Wheel of the Year, the seasons of your life
that repeat, have resonances, but are never the same.

How Pisces Are You?

The Sun is the hub around which the planets circle. Its gravity
pulls the planets to keep them in their courses and bends
space-time to create the place we call our solar system. The
Sun in your birth chart tugs on every other part of your chart
in a similar way. Everything is both bound and free, affected
but seeking its own direction. When people encounter
descriptions of Pisces traits, they will often begin to make
a list of which things apply to them and which don't. Some
will say that they are the epitome of Pisces traits, others will
claim that they are barely Pisces, and many will be somewhere
in between. Evaluating how closely or not you align with the
traditional characteristics of a Pisces is not a particularly
useful approach to understanding your sign. If you are a
Pisces, you have all the Pisces traits somewhere within you.
What varies from person to person is the expression of those
traits. Some traits express fully in a classic form, others are
blocked from expressing or are modified, and sometimes there
is a reaction to behave as the opposite of what is expected.
As a Pisces, and especially as a witch, you have the capacity

to activate dormant traits, to shape functioning traits, and to tone down overactive traits.

The characteristics and traits of signs are tendencies, drives, and affinities. Gravity encourages a ball to roll down a hill. A plant's leaves will grow in the direction of sunlight. The warmth of a fire will draw people together on a cold night. A flavor that you enjoy will entice you to take another bite of your food. Your Pisces Sun urges you to be and to act like a Pisces. That said, you also have free will and volition to make other choices. Moreover, the rest of your birth chart and the ever-changing celestial influences are also shaping your options, moods, and drives. The more you become aware of the traits and behaviors that come with being a Pisces, the easier it will be to choose how you express them. Most people want to have the freedom to explore themselves and make a difference in the world, but for a Pisces, it is essential for their well-being.

As a witch, you have additional tools to work with the Pisces energy. You can choose when to access and how you shape the qualities of Pisces as they come forth in your life. You can summon the energy of Pisces, name the traits you desire, and manifest them. You can also banish or neutralize or ground what you don't need. You can find where your Pisces energy short-circuits, where it glitches, and unblock it. You can examine your uncomfortable feelings and your less-than-perfect behaviors to seek the shadowed places within so you can heal or integrate them. Pisces is a spirit and a current of collective consciousness that is vast in size. Pisces is also a group mind and archetype. Pisces is not limited to humanity; it engages with plants, animals, minerals, and all the physical and nonphysical beings of the Earth and all its associated realms. As a witch, you can call upon and work with the spiritual entity that is Pisces. You can live your life as a ritual. The motion of your life can be a dance to the tune and rhythm of the heavens.

The Pisces Glyph

The glyph for Pisces is very simple to draw as it is two semicircles connected by a horizontal line, but its simplicity is an illusion. In some versions of the glyph, the horizontal line cuts through the semicircles, and in

others it stops, looking like a curvy capital *H*. In other versions, the two semicircles almost touch. In the pictographic code of the astrological glyphs, semicircles represent the arc of evolution, and a horizontal line is a conduit for meaning and motion. One of the semicircles faces left and the other faces right. The glyph for Pisces depicts duality and the desire for connection and union. The glyph implies expansion, but the semicircles also suggest that they are moving toward each other. The horizontal line is also where sea and sky meet at infinity's end. This work is about making the unknown visible and embracing and integrating all the parts of your being.

One of the symbols for Pisces is two fish swimming in opposite directions connected by a cord. This can be seen in the glyph. There is also an echo of Pisces's ruling planets: Neptune's trident and a rearranged version of Jupiter's glyph can be seen. Pisces rules the feet, and the glyph also reminds us that the two must act in harmony to walk, run, or swim. It can be seen as two antennas or two wavefronts approaching each other as well. You can see duality, polarity, triplicity, union, and more in this mutable glyph. It is Pisces's job to dive into the mysteries, and there are many in this glyph. The closer you look at the glyph and contemplate it, the more you see.

By meditating on the glyph, you will develop a deeper understanding of what it is to be a Pisces. You may also come up with your own personal myth or story about the glyph that can be a key that is uniquely yours. The glyph for Pisces can be used as a sigil to call or concentrate its power. The glyph for Pisces can be used in a similar fashion to the scribing of an invoking pentacle that is used to open the gates to the elemental realms. However, instead of the elemental realms, this glyph opens the way to the realm of emotions and mystical knowledge that is the source of Pisces. To make this glyph work, you need to deeply ingrain the feeling of scribing this glyph. Visually it is a simple glyph, so memorizing it is easy, but having a kinesthetic feel for it turns it into magick. Spend some time doodling the glyph on paper. Try drawing the glyph on your palm with a finger for several repetitions as that adds several layers of sensation and memory patterns.

Whenever you need access to more of your magickal energy, scribe the Pisces glyph in your mind, on your hand, in the air, however you can. Then pull, channel, and feel your center fill with whatever you need. It takes very little time to open this connection using the glyph. Consider making this one of the practices you use to get ready to do divination, spell work, or ritual, or just to start your day.

Pisces Patterns

This is a short list of patterns, guidelines, and predilections for Pisces Sun people to get you started. If you keep a book of shadows, or a journal, or files on a digital device to record your thoughts and insights on magickal work, you may wish to create your own list to expand upon these. The process of observing, summarizing, and writing down your own ideas in a list is a great way to learn about your sign.

- Pisces tend to connect with everyone and everything in their environment. Sensitivity in all its forms—physical, emotional, psychic, aesthetic, and so on—is your default setting.

- Compassion is your natural state of being, but often the state of the culture seems more than you can manage. This can cause strain and discomfort that can lead to growth or cause harm.

- You want to see past the surface of the world and understand the forces, forms, and essences that move and create reality. If this becomes an escape from the world, you won't find what you are seeking.

If it becomes your way to help this world by being a conduit between worlds, your development continues.

Meditation, art, music, and humanitarian work are some of the practices that keep you healthy and on an even keel. If you go numb, zone out, float off into spiritual la-la land, or self-medicate, then it is time to return to these or similar practices to regain clarity. The moments of your life are precious; be present in them.

The more you learn to laugh with the folly of the world, the kinder you'll be to others and to yourself. The more you encourage others to find the funny ways that things are connected together, the more friends and allies you'll have.

Pisces are sometimes thought to be impractical because they have so many dreams. However, when a Pisces commits to following their dreams, they are capable of astonishing accomplishments.

The spiritual power of water connects you to all planes of reality, of consciousness, of individuation, and oneness. This gives you access to psychic gifts that will affect your life whether you choose to embrace them or not.

The powerful emotions that Pisces feel draw them closer to people. The urge to go deep or to expand outward to touch the face of infinity is powerful. The desire to take refuge in their private fantasy world in the quiet of their room is also strong. The goal is to do all three in their optimal proportions.

Many will underestimate you because they think that sensitive means weak. Your emotional intelligence and intuition make you downright dangerous when pushed too hard.

Pity rarely serves a wholesome purpose. When you feel pity for others or yourself, take it as a sign to open that inner sight of yours and see that the divine spark is in everything. Then you'll know how to flip that emotion to fuel action that leads to good outcomes.

There are complicated polarities and currents that flow in a Piscean soul. You wish to evolve and become one with the universe. Paradoxically, to do this also requires separating and understanding each part of yourself so that you can create a better integration. Your divine spark, soul, spirit, body, mind, personality, individuality, place in your culture, and so on must be seen in their own light and context.

Other signs often are tagged as romantic. Pisces needs and wants Romance with a capital *R*. This can be bliss, but in that bliss and deep intimacy, make sure you do not lose yourself.

Confidence is like a muscle; the more you use it, the stronger it gets. Muscles often get sore when you give them a workout. So, when your self-confidence feels tender, it may be a good sign that you are building strength. Don't overthink it.

Pisces have the gift of accessing their whole life as needed. You can be the child full of wonder, the elder full of the wisdom of experience, and everything else in between.

If you are a witch, you are attracted to the other-worldly. But for a Pisces witch, the other worlds, the spirits, and the tingle of magickal power are as necessary as air, food, and water to their existence.

Like water, you can adjust your shape to accommodate most people and circumstances. This tends to attract friends and admirers, but they find it hard to see you. It is also harder for people to discover what you need and want from them. Reaffirm your boundaries to make it easier to be understood.

Mutable Water

The four elements come in sets of three. The modalities known as cardinal, fixed, and mutable are three different flavors or styles of manifestation for the elements. The twelvefold pattern that is the backbone of astrology comes from the twelve combinations produced from four elements times three modalities. As you go around the wheel of the zodiac, the order  of the elements is always fire, earth, air, then water, while the modalities are always in the order of cardinal, fixed, then mutable. Each season begins in the cardinal modality, reaches its peak in the fixed modality, and transforms to the next season in the mutable modality. The cardinal modality is the energy of creation bursting forth, coming into being, and spreading throughout the world. The fixed modality is the harmonization of energy so that it becomes and remains fully itself and is preserved. The mutable modality is the energy of flux that is flexibility, transformation, death, and rebirth.

Pisces is the twelfth sign in the zodiac, so it is water of the mutable modality that completes the whole cycle of the zodiac. This is why a Pisces witch can call up power to meld with different powers, planes, and states of consciousness so fully. As a Pisces witch, you can call upon water in all its forms, but it is easiest to draw upon mutable water.

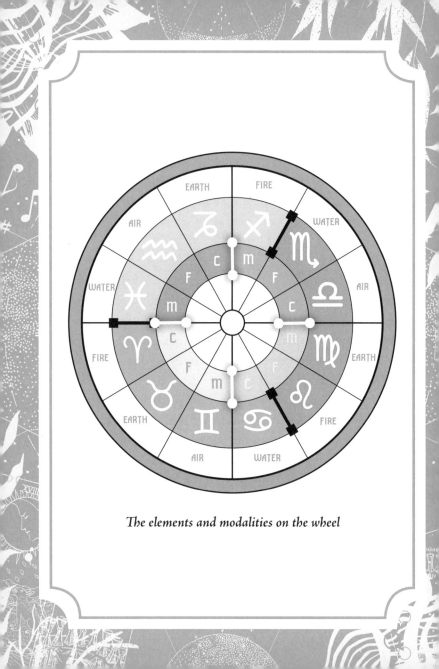

The elements and modalities on the wheel

Neptune, Your Ruling Planet

Your Sun sign determines the source and the type of energy that you have in your core. The ruling planet for a sign reveals your go-to moves and your intuitive or habitual responses for expressing that energy. Your ruling planet provides a curated set of prebuilt responses and custom-tailored stances for you to use in day-to-day life. Jupiter was the planet that was originally assigned to Pisces. In modern times, Neptune became assigned as its primary ruler. The name of this planet recalls the god of the wide sea. However, the planet Neptune and how it influences Pisces is more about the wide seas of consciousness, space, time, spirit, and so on. All the places and spaces where infinity and eternity circle back upon themselves are Neptune's domain. Since Pisces is a mutable water sign, this encourages the expressions of Neptune to include psychic gifts, empathy, emotional intelligence, mediumship, and a desire to walk the path of a mystic. Neptune is also the reason why Pisces must be careful not to abuse substances, zone out too often, dissociate from their day-to-day life, or stay ungrounded. It is easy for Pisces to ride the wave that never reaches the shore. Neptune's glyph is a trident, and it is a tool that resonates to the power of a Pisces witch. It is your secondary ruler of Jupiter that brings your drive to help people and build a better world. Your sense of hope is strongly connected to Jupiter.

Pisces witches are more strongly affected by whatever Neptune is doing in the heavens, and to a lesser degree Jupiter. It is useful to keep track of the aspects that Neptune is making with other planets. You can get basic information on what aspects mean and when they are happening in astrological calendars and online resources. You will feel Neptune retrogrades more strongly than most people, but you can find ways to make them useful periods to integrate what you have already experienced. Neptune moves slowly through the heavens, so most of the impact you feel will be through aspects made to faster-moving planets. However, when Jupiter in the heavens makes aspects to Neptune or sensitive spots in your natal chart, your magick changes in response to the nature of that aspect. You will also have a boost of power when the Sun is in the same degree as Neptune or Jupiter in your birth chart. Witches can shift their relationship with the powers that influence them. Your awareness of these powers makes it possible to harness those energies to purposes that you choose. Close your eyes, feel for that power, and channel it into your magick.

Neptune can be as great a source of energy for a Pisces witch as the element of water. Although there is some overlap between the qualities and capacities assigned to Neptune and water, the differences are significant. Neptune pushes you to expand until you merge with ever-expanding levels of consciousness and in so doing dilutes your personal feelings and identity as you approach the ultimate. Water is the medium of emotion and the keeper of personal meaning. Neptune governs your relationship to mysteries that are so vast they exceed your current shape and capacities. Water seeks the lowest point and takes on the shape and motion of all it encounters and summarizes its meaning. Neptune wants to foster evolution for you as an individual, us as a species, and for all beings. Water nurtures growth and brings about birth and rebirth so that lessons will be remembered. Neptune is the surface off which light can reflect to bring forth wisdom. Water is the principle of healing through cycles of the heart and contains the spirit of resilience. Over time, you can map out the overlapping regions and the differences between Neptune and water. Using both planetary and elemental resources can give you a much broader range and more finesse.

Pisces and the Zodiacal Wheel

The order of the signs in the zodiac can also be seen as a creation story where the run of the elements repeats three times. Pisces is in the last third of the zodiac and ends the final run of the four elements in the story of the universe. They are far from the start of creation; they are on the return journey to the source. The goal of the elements at this point of the story is to connect with the transpersonal and the collective. Pisces remembers their purposes for coming into being and the journey they have taken. The water of Pisces tries to understand itself, help others, and become one with their higher Self and cosmic consciousness. It evaluates what is within so that it might come to embrace their place as the ending of the unfolding story of personal and collective existence. Although Pisces is often stereotyped as too unfocused, sensitive, and ungrounded, the deeper truth is that they are in preparation to become their divine Self. Although true for all witches, the Pisces witch needs to accept themselves

The sign and planet rulers on the zodiac wheel

as they are, and walk with one foot on Earth and one foot in the otherworld. When you can consistently connect with your Pisces nature that is your core self, you become the power that brings about spiritual development in yourself and others. You can make progress in this quest through meditation and inner journeys, but that alone will not do. The Pisces witch learns by exploring their entire watery nature, opening to spirit, and then sharing their journey with others. When a Pisces witch does this, they become the intuitive whose words and actions shorten the distance between the worlds.

PISCES
CORRESPONDENCES

Power: To Believe

Keyword: Compassion

Roles: Intuitive, Dreamer, Mystic

Ruling Planet: Neptune with Jupiter as a secondary ruler

Element: Mutable Water

Colors: Turquoise, Seafoam, and All the Colors of the Sea

Shape: Dodecagon and Vesica Piscis

Metal: Platinum, Electrum, and Tin

Body Parts Ruled: Feet

Day of the Week: Thursday

Affirmation:
*When I am grounded in the Earth,
my spirit can soar higher*

WITCHCRAFT THAT COMES NATURALLY TO A PISCES

Mat Auryn

I understand that I might be seeing this through a subjective lens, but when it comes to the zodiac, it seems that the best was indeed saved for last, and that honor belongs to Pisces. As the final sign of the astrological wheel, Pisces encapsulates the culmination of all the preceding signs' strengths and qualities. We naturally embody a unique combination of empathy, psychism, intuition, and healing abilities that seemingly set us apart from the rest. Pisces witches, in particular, shine brightly as natural healers, with our deep understanding of emotions, our innate connection to the spiritual realms, and our capacity for compassion. So, what type of witchcraft and psychic ability comes naturally to a Pisces? All of it. This may sound a bit arrogant at first, but it's true. I haven't met a single Pisces witch or a witch with Pisces in their "Big Three" (Sun sign, Moon sign, rising sign) who wasn't incredibly psychic and magickal. We will excel in anything that engages the imagination directly (and many, if not all, magickal practices do), especially if there's an emotional charge to it. This makes Pisces predisposed to be a psychic witch, interacting with energy as psychic information and then being able to sculpt that energy with emotion, imagination, and willpower to cast our magick. Pisces also tend to be natural lucid dreamers, astral projectors, and spiritual mediums.

Pisces is hands down the natural mystic of the zodiac due to being both a water sign and a mutable sign. Being a water sign predisposes us to naturally being sensitive to emotions and energy, particularly the subtle realms of psychism, intuition, dreams, the astral, and spirit. Being a mutable sign gives us a transformative nature without solid boundaries. This mutability gives us flexibility that makes us shape-shifters; the merfolk, the selkies, and the melusines. While not physical, our shape-shifting ability permeates every other aspect of our being. We can effortlessly feel and match frequencies. When we learn to be conscious of our own energies, we can shift our brainwave states, our emotional states, and our spiritual frequency with ease in ways necessary for connection and direct experiences with psychism and the world of spirits. This makes Pisces fantastic spirit workers, whether a spirit guide, a familiar spirit, land spirits, the faeries, or almost any other type of spirit.

Archetypes and Deities

Pisces individuals often discover a deep connection with divine beings who embody distinct qualities such as compassion, healing, magick, dreaming, and prophecy. We're also drawn to deities that relate to depths, whether that's the ocean, the abyss, or the underworld. Here's a small sample of deities from across the world that seem to embody the archetypal energies that Pisces does. These explanations only scratch the surface of who these complex beings are. If any of these deities interest you, trust your intuition and let it serve as a stepping stone to begin research into the deity and the culture and tradition they come from, and remember to approach them with respect and sincerity.

- *Avalokiteshvara*—The compassionate embodiment of Mahayana Buddhism associated with empathy, mercy, and the alleviation of suffering—qualities aligned with Pisces energy.

- *Hekate*—Greek goddess of magick, witchcraft, and the Moon, invoked for protection during sleep, dream divination, and psychic abilities.

- *Isis*—Ancient Egyptian goddess associated with magick, healing, and intuition, embodying transformative power and emotional depth—ideal for Pisces.

💧 *Jesus Christ*—Christian figure known for love, compassion, healing, miracles, and selflessness; he's thought to symbolize the age of Pisces, and that's why there are so many fish themes in the New Testament.

💧 *Krishna*—Hindu incarnation of the divine associated with love, compassion, spiritual wisdom, inner transformation, and the unity of all beings—aligned with Pisces energy.

💧 *Manannán mac Lir*—Figure in Irish mythology representing the sea, dreams, and poetic inspiration, resonating with Pisces through mysticism and transformative water symbolism.

💧 *Morpheus*—Greek god of dreams, guiding individuals through the realm of dreams, offering insight, inspiration, and understanding of symbolic language to Pisces practitioners.

💧 *Oshun*—Yoruba deity associated with love, beauty, fertility, and healing, emphasizing compassion, emotional depth, and artistic expression—perfect for Pisces.

💧 *Poseidon/Neptune*—Greek and Roman gods of the sea, intuition, and the subconscious mind, reflecting the depths of emotions resonating with Pisces.

Quan Yin—East Asian bodhisattva known for compassion, mercy, healing, and the alleviation of suffering—a natural match for Pisces's empathetic nature.

Selene—Greek goddess of the Moon, embodying dreamy and ethereal qualities connected to intuition, dreams, and the mystical aspects of the lunar cycle, attracting many Pisces practitioners.

Yemaya—Deity in Santería associated with the ocean, maternal love, nurturing, and emotional healing, aligning with Pisces's nurturing and intuitive qualities.

Ritual Work—Lone Fish versus School of Fish

Our sign, ruled by Neptune, the planet of dreams and mysticism, grants us a unique approach to rituals and magick, enabling us to excel in both settings. Pisces individuals thrive in group settings that involve rituals, as our empathetic nature allows us to tap into the collective energy of the group. This connection makes it easier for us to commune with the spiritual realms, receive intuitive insights, and synchronize with the group mind of the coven or ritual participants. Moreover, the amplified energy generated in group rituals magnifies the effectiveness of our spells, divination, and manifestation work.
Being part of a ritual group provides

us with the opportunity to share and receive emotional support from like-minded individuals, which grounds, encourages, and validates our magickal practices. This support strengthens our confidence in our magickal endeavors and helps dispel any doubts we may have about the effectiveness of our spells or our personal magickal power. The combined energy of everyone involved in a group ritual creates a powerful synergy, enhancing the overall experience.

As Pisces Witches, practicing magick alone allows us to delve deep into our psyche, exploring our emotions, dreams, and intuitive insights without external distractions. When practicing solo, we enjoy the freedom to design rituals that align specifically with our unique spiritual needs and desires. This level of customization allows us to focus on our personal intentions and set a pace that resonates with our Piscean energy. Without the constraints of a group, we can embrace greater flexibility in our magickal practices. We can choose to perform rituals at the most opportune times, adapt them spontaneously, and experiment with various forms of magick without needing to conform to a collective structure. This grants us the freedom to become our own magickal innovators, capable of experimenting and adapting at our own whims, which can be more challenging within a group setting.

Scry Me a River

As Pisces, we possess inherent strengths that make us excellent psychics, mediums, and diviners, with a particular emphasis on our natural talent as seers and scryers. Our intuitive nature and heightened sensitivity provide us with an edge in perceiving and understanding the spiritual realm. We effortlessly tap into the subtle energies and vibrations that others might overlook, allowing us to grasp the unseen with ease. We possess a rich inner world that enables us to visualize and connect with various dimensions and realms. This gift of imagination allows us to access information beyond the physical realm, granting us the ability to see and sense things that many others cannot readily perceive. Openness and receptivity define us as Pisces. We embrace different perspectives and experiences, extending this attitude to the spiritual realm. We are open-minded, eagerly exploring and embracing our psychic abilities. Instead of dismissing intuitive insights or psychic phenomena as coincidences, we delve deeper into the unseen and unknown, enriching our understanding and expanding our psychic prowess. Our strength lies in our emotional intelligence.

We possess an empathetic understanding of emotions and an innate ability to empathize with others. This emotional depth enables us to tap into the energies and emotions surrounding a situation, providing valuable insights and guidance to those seeking answers. We are adept at reading between the lines and deciphering the unspoken, using our psychic abilities to offer clarity and support. The subconscious mind is our realm as Pisces, and we thrive in it. We possess a natural inclination to explore the depths of the psyche, making us skilled at deciphering hidden meanings and symbolism. Our connection to the subconscious allows us to access information and insights that lie beyond the conscious mind, enabling us to provide guidance and interpretations. Above all, our spiritual connection serves as a guiding force in our psychic abilities. We have a deep-rooted connection to the divine or higher realms. This connection fuels our intuition and psychic gifts, leading us to embrace practices such as meditation, energy work, and divination techniques. We constantly strive to enhance our psychic skills and expand our spiritual awareness, staying true to our innate abilities and spiritual calling.

Our imaginative nature as Pisces witches grants us a powerful tool for insight through scrying practices. Whether peering into crystal balls, observing shapes in smoke, transforming clouds, or deciphering patterns in nature's foliage, we enter a realm where our imagination intertwines with mystical energies. This imaginative exploration allows us to interpret visions, decode symbols, and extract profound revelations, transcending the physical realm. By embracing the beauty of these divination methods and combining our psychic abilities with the boundless power of our imagination, we gain access to a wealth of knowledge and wisdom. Through scrying, we unlock a gateway to symbolism, archetypes, and the collective consciousness. Our imagination thrives in these practices, providing a canvas for our faculties to divine freely. We transcend the mundane, weaving together the seen and unseen worlds, unraveling hidden meanings, and receiving profound guidance. By understanding that our imagination is a potent tool, not mere fantasy, we tap into the limitless wisdom of the universe. With this combination of imaginative exploration and psychic abilities, we navigate our spiritual path with confidence, accessing profound insights that guide us toward a deeper understanding of ourselves and the mysteries of life.

Swimming in the Sea of Dreams

We are also dreamers, often finding ourselves in the realm of the conceptual, fantasy, and idealism. For Pisces, magick performed within lucid dreams or in the astral realm can feel more natural to us, as we perform it outside of physical reality. This is also where we gain the most insight for psychic revelation, since we're at home in the realm of the subconscious mind, where imagination, psychism, and dreams emerge from. In many ways, we're sort of the aliens of the zodiac, being not only the last sign of the zodiac, but also a mutable one at that. This placement at the end of the zodiac is often seen as the man transforming to heightened spirit, the last step in spiritual evolution in the human's cycle of reincarnation. Our zodiacal symbol is two fish swimming in opposite directions with a fishing line tying the two together. One fish is said to represent being in the physical realm, while the other represents being in the world of spirit, and the difficulty is that they're swimming in different directions. This imagery can also be looked at as a fish astral projecting, with their silver cord connecting their physical body with their astral body.

Neptunian Eye Pillow

To really treat yourself to sweet dreams, try crafting this eye pillow. This eye pillow is filled with lavender, mugwort, and flaxseed and has practical and magickal benefits. On the practical level, it can be used to reduce stress and relax before bed, helping you fall asleep quicker and with a clearer mind. You can also warm it in the microwave (about twenty seconds) or cool it in the fridge or freezer to assist in relieving headaches. However, the magickal benefits are key here. Lavender, mugwort, and flaxseed create a synergy together that is used to increase mental powers, psychic visions, prophecies, and clarity of mind for activities like meditation. These three plant allies also ward against unwanted spirits and negative energies and enhance the quality and mood of one's dreams.

This eye pillow incorporates a sigil I've used for years for anything related to dream mysticism, whether that's magick, lucid dreaming, astral travel, or prophetic dream induction. It utilizes the glyph of Pisces and Neptune, an eye, and antennae.

Neptunian Eye Sigil

Instructions

Gently combine 2 cups of flaxseeds, ¼ cup of dried lavender, and ¼ cup of mugwort in your bowl. Once combined, gently stir until thoroughly mixed. Next, add 5 drops each of lavender and mugwort essential oils and gently stir a bit more until the essential oils have been distributed throughout. You have two options for creating an eye pillow: sewing one from fabric or filling a sock and tying the end. Either way, fill the pillow with your mix and draw the sigil on the outside of the fabric. Once the pillow is finished, envision the sigil (you can also look at the image of the sigil in the book while doing this). Hold your hands over the eye pillow and envision a fire burning electric blue and violet emitting from your hands and engulfing and activating the pillow. As you do, recite this charm:

> *Lavender, Mugwort, and Flaxseed,*
> *Lend your powers to this deed.*
> *Open the gates to the realm of dreams,*
> *Where prophetic wisdom ever gleams.*
> *Safe and secure, in the astral I fly,*
> *Ever lucid, as Neptune's azure eye.*

To use, simply place the pillow over your eyes while lying on your back as you drift to sleep.

MAGICAL
CORRESPONDENCES
Mat Auryn

Pisces magick is rooted in the realm of emotions, imagination, psychic abilities, trance work, meditation, mediumship, and dreaming. Pisces are naturally drawn to any magick involving liquid or water. After all, we are fish, swimming in the vast ocean of the cosmos. As mutable water signs, we possess the unique ability to transmute these subtle internal energies into something tangible and transformative.

Types of Spellcraft

- Energy healing
- Psychic/ intuition
- Dreamwork
- Visualization and manifestation
- Water magick
- Empathic spell work

Magical Tools

+ Chalice
+ Cauldron
+ Seashells
+ Divination tools
+ Teas and brews
+ Essential oils and tinctures

Magical Goals and Spell Ideas

+ Emotional healing and self-love
+ Intuition and psychic development
+ Shape-shifting and glamour spells
+ Spiritual connection and inner exploration
+ Manifesting dreams and creative projects
+ Astral projection and lucid dreaming

TIMING, PLACES, AND THINGS

Ivo Dominguez, Jr.

You've probably encountered plenty of charts and lists in books and online cataloging which things relate to your Sun sign and ruling planet. There are many gorgeously curated assortments of herbs, crystals, music playlists, fashions, sports, fictional characters, tarot cards, and more that are assigned to your Sun sign. These compilations of associations are more than a curiosity or for entertainment. Correspondences are like treasure maps to show you where to find the type and flavor of power you are seeking. Correspondences are flowcharts and diagrams that show the inner, occult, relationships between subtle energies and the physical world. Although there are many purposes for lists of correspondences, there are two that are especially valuable to becoming a better Pisces witch.

The first is to contemplate the meaning of the correspondences, the ways in which they reveal meaningful details about your Sun sign and ruling planet, and how they connect to you. This will deepen your understanding of what it is to be a Pisces witch. The second is to use these items as points of connection to access energies and essences that support your witchcraft. This will expand the number of tools and resources at your disposal for all your efforts.

Each of the sections in this chapter will introduce you to a type of correlation with suggestions on how to identify and use them. These are just starting points and you will find many more as you explore and learn more. As you broaden your knowledge, you may find yourself a little bit confused as you find that sources disagree on the correlations. These contradictions are generally not a matter of who is in error but a matter of perspective, cultural differences, and the intended uses for the correlations. Anything that exists in the physical world can be described as a mixture of all the elements, planets, and signs. You may be a Pisces, but depending on the rest of your chart, there may be strong concentrations of other signs and elements. For example, if you find that a particular herb is associated with both Pisces and Sagittarius, it is because it contains both natures in abundance. In the cases of strong multiple correlations, it is important that you summon or tune in to the one you need.

Times

You always have access to your power as a Pisces witch, but there are times when the flow is stronger, readily available, or more easily summoned. There are sophisticated astrological methods to select dates and times that are specific to your birth chart. Unless you want to learn quite a bit more astrology or hire someone to determine these for you, you can do quite well with simpler methods. Let's look at the cycles of the solar year, the lunar month, and the hours of day-night rotation. When the Sun is in Pisces, or the Moon is in Pisces, or it is the last of the night approaching dawn, you are in the sweet spot for tuning in to the core of your power.

Pisces season is roughly February 19 to March 20 but check your astrological calendar or ephemeris to determine when it is for a specific year in your time zone. The amount of energy that is accessible is highest when the Sun is at the same degree of Pisces as it is in your birth chart. This peak will not always be on your birth date but very close to it. Midway through Pisces season is another peak for all Pisces. Take advantage of Pisces season for working magick and for recharging and storing up energy for the whole year.

The Moon moves through the twelve signs every lunar cycle and spends around two and half days in each sign. When the Moon is in Pisces, you have access to more lunar power because the Moon in the heavens has a resonant link to the Sun in your birth chart. At some point during its time in Pisces, the Moon will be at the same degree as your Sun. For you, that will be the peak of the energy during the Moon's passage through Pisces that month. While the Moon is in Pisces, your psychism is stronger, as is your ability to manifest things. When the Moon is approaching the dark of the Moon, in any sign, you can draw upon its power more readily because this phase is resonant to your sign. Some Pisces are especially resonant to Jupiter's place in the heavens, so you may wish to track your experiences to see if this is true for you.

The peak of Pisces season at the midpoint, the fifteenth degree, is a day of peak mutability and a liminal space for your magick. You can look up when the Sun is in the fifteenth degree of Pisces for the current or future years using online resources or an ephemeris. Pisces is the twelfth sign of the zodiac, and the zodiac is like a clock for the purposes of spells and rituals. The two hours just before dawn resonate to the power of Pisces. If you are detail focused, you might be wondering when predawn begins. This varies with the time of year and with your location, but if you must have a time, think of it as 4:00 a.m. to 6:00 a.m. Or you can use your intuition and feel your way to when night has begun to change into day. Plan on using the Pisces energy of the night's last hours for inspiration and to feed spells for learning, divination, empowerment, and transformation.

The effect of these special times can be joined in any combination. For example, you can choose to do work at the end of night when the Moon or the Sun is in Pisces, or at the end of the night during the dark of the Moon in Pisces when it conjuncts the Sun in Pisces. Each of these time groupings will have a distinctive feeling. Experiment and use your instincts to discover how to use these in your work.

Places

There are activities, professions, phenomena, and behaviors that have an affinity, a resonant connection, to Pisces and its ruling planet, Neptune. These activities occur in the locations that suit or facilitate their expressions. There is magick to be claimed from those places that is earmarked for Pisces or your ruling planet, Neptune. Just like your birth chart, the world around you contains the influences of all the planets and signs, but in different proportions and arrangements. You can always draw upon Pisces or Neptune energy, though there are times when it is more abundant depending on astrological considerations. Places and spaces have energies that accumulate and can be tapped like a battery. Places contain the physical, emotional, and spiritual environments that are created by the actions of the material objects, plants, animals, and people occupying those spaces. Some of the interactions between these things can generate or concentrate the energies and patterns that can be used by Pisces witches.

If you look at traditional astrology books, you'll find listings of places assigned to Pisces and Neptune that include locations such as these:

- 💧 On the ocean or a large lake where land can't be seen.

- 💧 Places where occult, metaphysical, or devotional activities occur.

- 💧 Hidden gardens, labyrinths, and outdoor spaces created to be spiritual.

- 💧 Astronomical observatories and scenic lookouts.

- 💧 Wherever people are entranced by music or art.

These are very clearly linked to the themes associated with Pisces and Neptune. With a bit of brainstorming and free-associating, you'll find many other less obvious locations and situations where you can draw upon this power. For example, whenever spiritual teachers, energy healers, improvisational artists, or psychics are at work, they can produce a current that you can plug into. Any situation where you use your imagination or intuition to reveal deeper realities or bridges between worlds can become a source of power. All implements or actions related to divination, magick, and activities that shift your consciousness could also be sources for energy.

While you can certainly go to places that are identified as locations where Pisces and/or Neptune energy is plentiful to do workings, you can find those energies in many other circumstances. Don't be limited by the idea that the places must be the ones that have a formalized link to Pisces. Be on the lookout for Pisces or Neptune themes and activities wherever you may be. Remember that people thinking, feeling, or participating in activities connected to your sign and its ruling planet are raising power. If you can identify with it as resonating with your Sun sign or ruling planet, then you can call the power and put it to use. You complete the circuit to engage the flow with your visualization, intentions, and actions.

Plants

Pisces seeks elevated states of consciousness and immersing their awareness in their senses. The colors associated with Pisces are all the colors of the sea and all soft soothing hues. Neptune opens the psychic senses, expands consciousness, dulls consciousness, and elevates or intoxicates. Herbs, resins, oils, fruits, vegetables, woods, and flowers that strongly exhibit one or more of these qualities can be called upon to support your magick. Here are a few examples:

- Brahmi (water hyssop) helps brighten your consciousness.
- Lotus (especially blue) opens your higher senses.

- Lobelia helps distinguish wholesome spirits from unfriendly ones.

- Elecampane to commune with nature spirits.

- Irish moss for abundance, luck, and protection.

Once you understand the rationale for making these assignments, the lists of correspondences will make more sense. Another thing to consider is that each part of a plant may resonate more strongly with a different element, planet, and sign. Brahmi shows its connection with Pisces and Neptune with its capacity to prepare consciousness for higher planes. However, Brahmi is also an herb of Virgo and Mercury because it can also sharpen the mind for mundane tasks. Which energy steps forward depends on your call and invitation. Like calls to like is a truism in witchcraft. When you use your Pisces nature to make a call you are answered by the Pisces part of the plant.

Plant materials can take the form of incense, anointing oils, altar pieces, potions, washes, magickal implements, foods, flower arrangements, and so on. The mere presence of plant material that is linked to Pisces or Neptune will be helpful to you. However, to gain the most benefit from plant energy, you need to actively engage with it.

Push some of your energy into the plants and then pull on it to start the flow. Although much of the plant material you work with will be dried or preserved, it retains a connection to living members of their species. You may also want to reach out and try to commune with the spirit, the group soul, of the plants to request their assistance or guidance. This will awaken the power slumbering in the dried or preserved plant material. Spending time with living plants, whether they be houseplants, in your yard, or in a public garden will strengthen your conversation with the green beings under Pisces's eye.

Crystals and Stones

Before digging into this topic, let's clear up some of the confusion around the birthstones for the signs of the zodiac. There are many varying lists for birthstones. Also be aware that some are related to the calendar month rather than the zodiacal signs. There are traditional lists, but the most commonly available lists for birthstones were created by jewelers to sell more jewelry. Also be cautious of the word *traditional* as some jewelers refer to the older lists compiled by jewelers as "traditional." The traditional lists created by magickal practitioners also diverge from each other because of cultural differences and the availability of different stones in the times and places the lists were created. If you have already formed a strong connection to a birthstone that you discover is not really connected to the energy of your sign, keep using it. Your connection is proof of its value to you in moving, holding, and shifting energy, whether or not it is specifically attuned to Pisces.

These are my preferred assignments of birthstones for the signs of the zodiac:

Aries	Bloodstone, Carnelian, Diamond
Taurus	Rose Quartz, Amber, Sapphire
Gemini	Agate, Tiger's Eyes, Citrine
Cancer	Moonstone, Pearl, Emerald
Leo	Heliodor, Peridot, Black Onyx
Virgo	Green Aventurine, Moss Agate, Zircon
Libra	Jade, Lapis Lazuli, Labradorite
Scorpio	Obsidian, Pale Beryl, Nuummite
Sagittarius	Turquoise, Blue Topaz, Iolite
Capricorn	Black Tourmaline, Howlite, Ruby

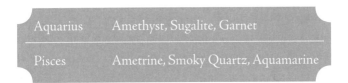

Aquarius	Amethyst, Sugalite, Garnet
Pisces	Ametrine, Smoky Quartz, Aquamarine

There are many other possibilities that work just as well, and I suggest you find what responds best for you as an individual. I've included all twelve signs in case you'd like to use the stones for your Moon sign or rising sign. Hands-on experimentation is the best approach, so I suggest visiting crystal or metaphysical shops and rock and mineral shows when possible. Here's some information on the three that I prefer for Pisces.

Ametrine

Ametrine is a naturally occurring blend of amethyst and citrine. It has all the qualities of both its constituents and exemplifies the proper use and balance of dualities that is one of Pisces's challenges. This is highly valuable for a Pisces seeking serenity. It also encourages an open mind and creativity and bolsters your vitality when doing spiritual or magickal work. It supports both your solar plexus chakra and your crown chakra to keep you lucid as you work your magick. Ametrine is also known for aiding self-confidence and helping you let go of intrusive negative thoughts. This stone helps harmonize group rituals or group healing efforts.

Smoky Quartz

This is one of the best stones to encourage grounding without closing down any of the psychic senses. That is reason enough to add it to your collection. Smoky quartz helps you process stressful and negative experiences so that they turn into emotional muscle rather than scar tissue. It helps foster your sense of security and belief in your capacity to persevere. It also helps keep energy attachments and astral debris from getting stuck in your aura. When you wear it or keep it near you, it helps clear away or repel static, negative atmospheres and energy clutter. The cairngorm variant of smoky quartz is also good as protection against intentionally spiteful energy or beings.

Aquamarine

This gem has a history of being used to protect sailors at sea from storms, waves, and attackers. Aquamarine was also a homing beacon to get back to home port safely. For a Pisces, it offers protection when moving through the seas of time and space and spirit. Aquamarine will help you back to your body and the here and now when your work is done. This crystal helps improve psychic gifts, especially clairvoyance, by assisting you in sorting the details you pick up into their proper order. Aquamarine helps you remember your true shape, energy, and boundaries and return to them. This is invaluable after shape-shifting, doing divination for others, or group ritual work.

Intuition and spiritual guidance play a part in the making of correlations and, in the case of traditional lore, the collective experience of many generations of practitioners. There is also reasoning behind how these assignments are made, and understanding the process will help you choose well. Here are some examples of this reasoning:

- Crystals assigned to Pisces are often pale blue, seafoam, or watery mixes that remind us of Neptune. Mother-of-pearl and turquoise are good examples of these.

- Pisces metals are platinum and blends of metals that shine, such as electrum. Stones that contain these will be expensive and are uncommon. You will find platinum aura (also called angel or opal aura) quartz. This is quartz with a very thin layer of platinum deposited on its surface. These are helpful but beware as there are many fakes.

- Crystals or stones such as pearls, celestite, moldavite, and blue kyanite whose lore and uses are related to Pisces or Neptune or Jupiter actions or topics, such as soul flight, spiritual

evolution, and peace, are recommended for
Pisces.

🜄 Crystals that are the opposite of the themes for
Pisces provide a counterbalance to an excessive
manifestation of Pisces traits. For example,
carnelian is on lists of crystals for many other
signs but is useful for Pisces because it provides
vitality for grounded actions.

🜄 Crystals suggested for Virgo, your opposite sign,
are also useful to maintain your balance. Moss
agate is a good example of this principle.

Working with Ritual Objects

A substantial number of traditions or schools of witchcraft use
magickal tools that are consecrated to represent and hold the
power of the elements. Oftentimes in these systems, there is
one primary tool for each of the elements and other tools that
are alternatives to these or are mixtures of elements. There are
many possible combinations and reasons for why the elements
are assigned to different tools in different traditions,
and they all work within their own context. Find and
follow what works best for you. Magickal tools and
ritual objects are typically cleansed, consecrated,
and charged to prepare them for use. In addition
to following whatever procedure you may have

for preparing your tools, add in a step to incorporate your energy and identity as a Pisces witch. This is especially productive for magickal tools and ritual objects that are connected to water or are used to store, direct, or focus power. By adding Pisces energy and patterning into the preparation of your tools, you will find it easier to raise, move, and shape energy with them in your workings.

There are many magickal tools and ritual objects that do not have any attachment to specific elements. The core of your life force and magickal power springs from your Pisces Sun. So, when you consciously join your awareness of your Pisces core with the power flowing through the tools or objects, it increases their effectiveness. Adding your watery energy does not make it a water tool, it makes it a Pisces tool tuned to you. Develop the habit of using the name *Pisces* as a word of power, the glyph of Pisces for summoning power, and the blue-greens and soft clear colors of Pisces to visualize its flow. Whether it be a pendulum, a wand, a crystal, or a chalice, your Pisces energy will be quick to rise and answer your call.

A Charging Practice

When you consciously use your Pisces witch energy to send power into tools, it tunes them more closely to your aura. Here's a quick method for imbuing any tool with your Pisces energy.

1. Place the tool in front of you on a table or altar.

2. Take a breath in, imagining that you are breathing in blue-green energy, and then say "Pisces" as you exhale. Repeat this three times.

3. Bring your feet together. Depending on whether you are standing or seated, you will do this differently. Look down at your feet and imagine that each foot is on top of a semicircle of blue-green energy. Now slowly separate your feet and see a line of blue-green energy connecting the semicircles. You've just formed the glyph for Pisces with the part of the body it rules.

4. Now using a finger, trace the glyph of Pisces over or on the tool you are

charging. Repeat this several times and imagine the glyph being absorbed by the tool.

5. Pick up the tool, take in a breath while imaging blue-green energy, then blow that charged breath over the tool.

6. Say "Blessed be!" and proceed with using the tool or putting it away.

Hopefully this charging practice will inspire you and encourage you to experiment. Develop the habit of using the name *Pisces* as a word of power, the glyph for Pisces for summoning power, and the watery colors of Pisces to visualize its flow. Feel free to use these spontaneously. Whether it be a pendulum, a wand, a crystal, a chalice, a ritual robe, or anything else that catches your imagination, these simple methods can have a large impact. The Pisces energy you imprint into objects will be quick to rise and answer your call.

HERBAL
CORRESPONDENCES

♓

These plant materials all have a special connection to your energy as a Pisces witch. There are many more, but these are a good starting point.

Herbs	
Mugwort	to strengthen psychic senses
Skullcap	for healing auric wounds and binding promises
Willow	for renewal, rebirth, and growth

Flowers

Gardenia	for easing harsh emotions, especially heartache
Lavender	for clarity and wisdom
Hyacinth	to understand the beauty of the world

Incense and Fragrances

Ylang-ylang	to attract love and joy
Camphor	to cleanse or to call power
Vanilla	for warming the heart and your home

CLEANSING AND SHIELDING

Mat Auryn

Pisces are known for their sensitivity, both emotionally and energetically. As such, we tend to absorb things around us since we naturally want to process things internally. Often, we function as sponges, whether we want to or not. This sensitivity often makes us fantastic psychics and intuitives, but this absorption of everything can also be very detrimental to us. We can quickly become overwhelmed by our environments and the people within them. Large, noisy crowds can sometimes feel like torture to a Pisces, especially if it's an emotionally charged area. Likewise, being around people expressing a strong emotion can cause the Pisces to start taking on those emotions themselves and confusing them for their own. Consistent cleansing and shielding are crucial for a Pisces's well-being, making it potentially more important for them than for other signs, given their sensitivity. Due to this heightened sensitivity, a Pisces's well-being relies heavily on consistent cleansing and shielding.

Keeping Your Inner and Outer Ponds Clean

When it comes to cleansing, a key for Pisces is to think in terms of emotion and water imagery. We are the only zodiac sign, with our symbol being the two fish, where water is always necessary. The other two water signs, Cancer the crab and Scorpio the scorpion, although they are also emotional signs, have the ability to transition between land and water like animals. Unlike them, fish cannot survive without water. Therefore, it is crucial to maintain cleanliness within our inner emotional energy, our "water," as well as the energy in the external environment where we spend most of our time. Since our sign is mutable, I've found that other Pisces and I tend to do well with that quality, which is one of transmutation, of changing something into something else. This means that when it comes to cleansing, we're naturally more talented at transforming energy than we might be at chasing it away. Aside from the following techniques, consider cleansing with sound, such as uplifting and soothing instrumental music or playing a crystal singing bowl. Music stirs our souls and helps us unconsciously tap into our psychic abilities. As such, not only will the sound help clear the space by elevating its vibration, but you'll also be able to help push it along by willing the energy to transmute due to the evocative effect music and sound have upon us.

The Waters of Purity

The following is my simplified version of the Kala rite, which I originally learned from another Pisces, Storm Faerywolf. The Kala rite is a foundational practice in the Faery/Feri tradition of witchcraft, which is a ritual of cleansing and transforming energy. Rather than releasing your blockages and adverse mental and emotional energy, the Kala rite allows you to transmute it into something that empowers and heals you. Water is used as a conduit for this energy transformation and cleansing. You could think of this in terms of conditioning the water for a fishbowl. What I mean by that is that you can't just add tap water into it when you have a pet fish. Instead, the water must be treated with special chemicals that neutralize harmful agents and transform the water into a safe and healthy quality for your fish. That is what we are doing with this exercise. It's all the same emotional and energetic water within us; we're just purifying it through the power of transmutation instead of getting rid of it.

Instructions:

Begin by filling a glass with drinking water. Hold it against your belly. Then, begin breathing with emphasis on your exhalations. As you do this, direct your breath and will to release any negative feelings, psychic disturbances, and internal blockages, envisioning them like dark smoke or a toxic sludge entering the water between your hands.

Next, you will call upon the power of the divine, the spirit that composes all of reality yet transcends all of existence. Raise your glass of water to your third eye between your brows. Call out,

You who transmute all things, Spirit Divine of old,
Lend your power to this glass of water that I hold.
Take all my pain, my stress, and what now ills me,
Transforming this water into a remedy that heals me.

Envision a divine lightning bolt of electric blue power striking the glass of water. As it does, it instantly transforms all the smoky watery sludge into a vibrant and pristine glass of water glowing with white and electric blue energy. Now drink the full glass of water at once, envisioning the energetic charge of divine transmutation that the water holds, entering your body and absorbing into every cell of your body.

Pisces Purifying Room Spray

The following is a room spray that I've crafted with the intent of cleansing a space (or your aura) tailored explicitly to Pisces's traits. The focus of the oil is to cleanse in a manner that doesn't just erase or chase away the energy of a room but instead transforms it by elevating its vibration while simultaneously heightening your natural psychic and intuitive faculties. The energy of this spray is soothing, and despite all its floral ingredients, it doesn't smell as flowery as you'd expect. Instead, it has a very mystical, refreshing, and dreamy fragrance. So trust me when I say you gotta try this!

You will need:

- 2-ounce spray bottle
- Camphor essential oil
- Jasmine essential oil
- Lavender essential oil
- Lily essential oil
- Lotus essential oil
- Palmarosa essential oil
- Spearmint essential oil
- Opium fragrance oil (optional but highly recommended)

- ✦ A tiny tumbled piece of amethyst (optional but highly recommended)
- ✦ Witch hazel alcohol
- ✦ Water

Instructions:

If you're using the optional amethyst, simply hold it in your hand and imagine it glowing while directing your willpower and intention toward it. Amethyst is ruled by Pisces and is a stone of intuition, serenity, and balance. It also assists in healing addictive qualities we may have, whether that's substances, emotions, or ideas. Those attributes make it perfect for a Pisces cleansing spray, as it directly addresses one of the shadow qualities of a Pisces while promoting a balanced and psychic environment. Mentally ask the crystal to bring those to the blend. Then, place the stone in the two-ounce spray bottle.

Next, simply add the essential oils one by one. This recipe calls for five drops of each oil. As you add the oil, connect with the plant spirit of each by saying something along the lines of,

> *I call to the spirit of (specific essential oil) to empower this blend that will cleanse a space as I intend.*

After adding all your oils, add a splash of witch hazel (think along the lines of what would fill a thimble), then fill the rest with water. Place your spray cap on the top, and shake it up a bit once secured tightly. For larger spray bottle sizes, just do the math based on this recipe's rule: five drops each per every two ounces of water. Spray in a room or around your aura when you need it to be transmuted to an energy that is conducive to your Piscean nature.

Ugh! Boundaries!

While boundaries are always the best form of protection, that can pose a difficulty for us as Pisces. Pisces naturally have a hard time with boundaries due to our empath nature. So while personal solid and energetic boundaries are essential, this poses more of a struggle for us than it might for other signs. If we think of our symbol of the fish as a metaphor, this makes complete sense because there aren't often any clear boundaries within the water. So while direct blocking may take extra work for us to develop, there are energy techniques that can be easier for us where we are taking more of an evasive approach as opposed to the more traditional shielding stance of energetic protection.

Celestial Waterfall of Protection

Since we have a hard time not absorbing our surrounding environment, even when we try to shield ourselves from it, we're bound to take some of it on more than other people. This simple energy technique calls upon your higher Self, the divine, perfect, and powerful soul component that watches over us. The technique will help you by not trying to resist and block energies but by having it quickly flush out of your personal space.

For this technique, simply close your eyes, take a few deep breaths, and try to relax as much as possible. Once you're relaxed and focused, bring your attention to a few feet above your head. First, visualize your higher Self as a luminous star (like a glowing orb, not like a pentagram) glowing with the thrums of divine power and authority. The star is beautiful and pure white but has an iridescent quality, shimmering with bits of the colors of the rainbow. Next, visualize it rising even higher, about ten feet above the crown of your head. Finally, the star begins sending a liquid white opalescent light that flows down with the intensity of a waterfall. As it comes down, imagine that it has not only the powerful sound of water rushing, but also the sound of a heavenly choir.

Now recite the following charm with feeling. Feel every word you say, like you truly mean it, with every bit of your emotional body.

By the Celestial waters rushing down
By the Celestial waters that surround
What isn't mine cannot stay
What isn't mine will flow away
Discordant energies that aren't right
Flush right through with speed and might
I will not absorb what does not belong
I cascade it away by Witch Soul's song

Feel the truth of the words that you just spoke into existence. Then, keep the visualization of the waterfall of liquid light within your mind's eye for just a few more moments, then release the visualization, knowing that it's still performing its job without your attention.

Army of Me Evasive Technique

One of the first shielding techniques I was taught was to envision mirrors around you reflecting unbalanced energy away from you and back toward its source. While this isn't an inherently faulty technique, this can pose a problem for a Pisces (or anyone who is super sensitive) as this tends to create an energetic feedback loop where the energy just keeps building and building around you as it bounces back and forth, amplifying each time. Eventually, those shields are not going to be strong enough. However, we can take this idea and modify it to better suit Pisces. Instead of shields of mirrors, an energetic "hall of mirrors" works better for us. Think of the trope in movies when someone is chasing another person in a hall of mirrors. They can see the other person, but they have no idea which is the real one! That is one of the main ideas behind this approach.

As mentioned, Pisces's primary defense isn't directly interacting with and combating energy. Our true defensive power lies in evasion, illusion, confusion, and misdirection. This is another reason the fish is a perfect symbol for us. Fish are commonly known to swim in schools. The school of fish reacts and responds intuitively in a way scientists still haven't figured out. Two main reasons fish swim in schools are to create an illusion of being a much larger singular fish and to create safety in numbers. The more eyes on the lookout for predators and other threats, the stronger the chance of evading them. The logic and purpose of this shielding are based on that idea.

Close your eyes and take a deep relaxing breath. Next, pull up the screen of your mind's eye. Envision a holographic mirror image of yourself facing outward before, behind, and on both sides of you. Now envision more of these replicas between them so that you have one to the north, northeast, east, southeast, south, southwest, west, and northwest in correlation to you. Think of it like being surrounded by bodyguards who look like clones of yourself. Keep surrounding yourself with more layers of these energy holograms of yourself until you feel like you're in the middle of a crowd of them.

Now recite the following verbally or mentally with feeling and meaning to program these energy doubles:

An army of me, I now deploy
Serve me well as my decoys.
Energies that come to harm and abuse

You will misdirect and confuse.
Take the hit for me as my masquerade
Alerting me of threats that I may evade.

That's it! They have their instructions. Open your eyes, ground yourself, and just keep swimming, little fish!

WHAT SETS A PISCES OFF, AND HOW TO RECOVER

Mat Auryn

When we're triggered as Pisces, our instinct is to withdraw. We aren't ones for direct conflict, and the more we're set off, the less direct we will be and the more we will distance ourselves. This can come out as passive-aggressiveness, giving "the silent treatment," taking a break from someone, or cutting them off entirely from your life. Sometimes withdrawing from a person or situation is exactly what we need to do, but many times it's not. Learning to discern when it is and isn't proper to do so can be a struggle. Often our reactions and responses to things cause the issues to snowball until they're out of our control, becoming worse than they initially were. As Pisces witches, we want to master our emotions so they don't master us. Learning how to interact with other people and our emotions is crucial for survival.

Something essential for us to learn as Pisces witches is that other people aren't coming from the same place we are. We have this natural tendency to be naïve with other people. We often try to find the best in them and assume that since we come from a good place and want to see others well, they will do the same for us; but this doesn't mean that this is how other people operate. This is the biggest lesson a Pisces can learn and one I constantly have to relearn myself. Instead of seeing others through rose-colored glasses, try to see them for who they are. Then, we can seek to understand why someone behaves the way they do and where their suffering stems from without tolerating toxic behavior.

We can establish healthy boundaries while understanding that a person is unwell or wounded, and having sympathy and empathy for that is our eternal balancing act. My motto has been to wish those sorts of people well, but in a different well than my own. We can have compassion for another person without becoming a doormat. We must learn to see the best in someone as well as their flaws from previous wounds without condoning or enabling their toxicity within our own lives. This is helpful to keep in mind as we explore our triggers and how to recover from them.

Insensitivity

Insensitivity is the cardinal sin in a Pisces's mind. As incredibly emotional and sensitive people, we know that delivery with consideration of how someone feels is important. Bluntness and harsh truths can be worse than lying to us. However, we recognize that the truth doesn't have to be harsh to be the truth; it can be gentle and considerate while still being the truth. We are so overly cautious with the emotional delivery that we are often mistaken for being manipulative due to our expectation that the other person has enough emotional intelligence to read between the lines. Often, we discover that they can't. This can also come out in interesting ways when we're upset with someone and want them to understand without direct confrontation. Pisces are fluent speakers of passive-aggressiveness when upset, adding to the misconception of Pisces being manipulative.

Recognizing that directness is often valued in communication is critical. Most people don't mean to be insensitive or harsh, and it's important to remind ourselves of that. Unfortunately, there are cases where we find out they intend to hurt someone's feelings, whether that's us or someone else—especially if it's someone we love. This is a case when learning personal boundaries comes back into the picture. Interacting with toxic people in your life can quickly poison you. Establish firm boundaries of what isn't acceptable behavior and most importantly, enforce them! Remember that a boundary isn't a boundary unless it's enforced. This is the most crucial form of directness in which a Pisces can engage. If your or another person's feelings are being intentionally hurt, it is probably time for you to swim away from that intentionally insensitive individual.

Don't Rain on Our Parade

We are huge dreamers and, when excited about something, are incredibly optimistic about it. When someone rains on our parade by being pessimistic about something we're excited and optimistic about, it can feel like a personal attack. This can feel so intense that it feels like the person isn't just attacking us but our whole paradigm. The Pisces witch often understands the power of the mind and emotions for manifesting and will often employ the power of positive thinking. When someone shows doubt or tries to explain why something is unrealistic, it can feel like they're battling our powers of manifestation.

There are a few things to consider here. As Pisces, we are potent manifesters when our thoughts, emotions, imagination, and will are united. Unfortunately, we're an incredibly naïve sign as well. It's important to reflect on whether we're manifesting or if we're spiritually bypassing and gaslighting ourselves.

Understanding that the other person isn't trying to attack us or our paradigm is paramount. Perhaps they have a critical insight worth considering. Or, perhaps, you need to safeguard your frequency, vibration, emotions, optimism, and enthusiasm. I cannot tell you how many times someone has told me something was impossible or tried to rain on my parade with something I was manifesting, only to prove them wrong. Due to this, it's often best to keep your excitement for something you're manifesting utterly secret until it has manifested. Often for us, less doubt is less resistance.

Don't Tell Us How to Feel

This ties into the last one. Having someone tell us to change our mood can boil our blood, even if the person is well-meaning and just trying to cheer us up. Invalidating and dismissing our feelings will often only worsen the situation for us. As Pisces witches, it's not only okay to feel how we're feeling, but it's imperative for our well-being. Give yourself some alone time to process your feelings and explore your emotions. However, we need to learn to recognize when we aren't processing those feelings anymore but instead basking in them. We can get lost in our emotions if we aren't careful. There comes a point when we're just wallowing in self-pity and martyrdom, which is a sign that it's time to shift our focus to something else to make us feel better and change our mood.

Criticism

When Pisces is asking for feedback, we often aren't *really* asking for it unless we're asking about a specific detail. Pisces do not handle criticism well, especially when it's related to our creative endeavors. We gobble up positive reinforcement, praise, and compliments like koi at feeding time. Throw on top of the fact that we're incredibly sensitive, and criticism (especially unsolicited) can feel like the person is invalidating who we are. When someone gives us criticism, it needs to be highly constructive and sandwiched in positivity. It's important to remember that when you ask for thoughts and feedback about something, the other person probably assumes you mean exactly what you're asking. So don't ask if you don't want to *really* hear the feedback. A better approach is just saying, "Hey, check out this thing I made." That will often curb any criticism you may not be prepared to hear.

Close-Minded and Overly Skeptical Folks

The traditional planetary ruler of Pisces is Jupiter, which gives us an expansive nature, especially in the realms of spirituality and religion. Our modern planetary ruler is Neptune, considered a higher vibration of Jupiter; it rules mystical experiences, things not being what they appear, and the absence of boundaries. This paired with Pisces being a mutable sign means that for us, anything and everything is possible in the universe, particularly when it's metaphysical. As a result, we can often hold contradictory ideas as simply examples or models, pointing to a greater truth in ways that often baffle other people who want things to be clearly defined, neatly boxed, and logical. As such, we can be seen as dismissive of science, especially when it contradicts anything related to our beliefs about spirituality.

A closed mind is an atrocity to us, but it's vital to understand that we can sometimes be naïve and prone to fall into illusion and delusion. The best way to approach this as a Pisces is to take a holistic approach to the world. Recognize that science and medicine have their place and need not be abandoned just because we also believe in spiritual approaches. I have seen many Pisces witches neglect logic, science, and medicine because they may be critical or skeptical of our spiritual ideas and approaches. It's important to realize that this is a form of close-mindedness as well. Remember that the alchemist utilized what we'd call today traditional science with spirituality to achieve the miraculous. This tempered approach will keep us on the right track, where we don't deny either science or the metaphysical.

Three Uses for the Impressionability of Water

Thealandrah

I'm sharing three practices that make use of how water easily accepts vibrational imprints. Recognition leads to connection and cooperation. Energy follows focus. When we exercise and place our attention on the muscle group being worked, we get better results. This is also true in etheric or astral spaces. Recognize water within and without.

You will need:

+ A glass of water
+ An enhydro quartz crystal
+ Sea salt

Instructions:

To begin the working, say,

> *I am 70 percent water.*
>
> *I live within the body of the being Earth whose surface is three quarters water.*
>
> *I invite the element of water to step forward and be consciously present within me.*
>
> *I invite the Intelligence of water to step forward and be consciously present within me.*

The first practice is to charge at least one glass daily for yourself. Holding your hand over the glass, speak the blessing or affirmation of your choice, such as,

> *I call to the Light of life to infuse this water. May it bring me good health and well-being.*

Consciously drink deeply. It may also be used to pour libations. Charge the water you cook with in the same way. Be aware that you may unconsciously affect water depending on the strength of the emotion you are holding while cooking. You may as well do it consciously with a chosen purpose. Consider charging the water or coffee provided at meetings.

For the second practice, get an enhydro quartz crystal. Clear it to prep it for this purpose. Wait for the next steady rain, a gentle cleansing, replenishing rain without thunder or lightning. You may be indoors or outside in the rain. Center and ground yourself. Use the recognition above or similar words of your choice. Sense the waters of your body rise and respond to you. Expand your awareness through your whole self. Next, allow the rain to flow through your levels of self, from the most liminal to the physical. Sense the rain washing away that which is no longer needed. Take your enhydro crystal in your hand and ask it to *store* this experience of an astral cleansing rain. Hold the request and the crystal until the experience has been accepted by the crystal, then put it down. Release your awareness of both the rain and your body's water. Use this crystal as a quick personal energy reset by holding it and calling up its cleansing rain energy after challenging conversations or after work before entering your home.

The third practice uses sea salt to heighten the programming of water in mister bottles to clear spaces without scent or smoke. Call to the being or deity you work with. Ask them to program the salt crystals with light that repels all that is not in accordance with light, life, love, and law or words to that effect. Spray your office, treatment room, hospital room, and so on as needed.

The impressionability of water is both an asset to us as magick workers and a vulnerability. Respect and conserve the water we have available to us. Recognize that how we manage water affects the being Earth, and all the beings who reside within her.

A BRIEF BIO OF SYBIL LEEK: BRITAIN'S MOST FAMOUS WITCH

* * *

Patricia Lafayllve

Sybil Leek (1922–1982) called herself "an ordinary witch from the New Forest, England."[2] She was from Stoke-on-Trent, in Staffordshire, and claimed that her family had been in witchcraft since 1134. She had an ancestor, Molly Leigh, who died in 1746 after being accused of witchcraft. After publishing her autobiography, *Diary of a Witch*, the BBC labelled Sybil Leek "Britain's most famous witch."[3]

Leek began writing after Britain's witchcraft laws were repealed in 1951. A prolific author, she published over sixty books. She called her family's religion "Traditional Witchcraft" and in a 1966 radio broadcast defined the religion as "a belief in

2. Walter H. Waggoner, "Sybil Leek, 'Ordinary Witch from New Forest,' Dies at 65," *The New York Times*, October 29, 1982, https://www.nytimes.com/1982/10/29/obituaries/sybil-leek-ordinary-witch-from-new-forest-dies-at-65.html.
3. Sara Odeen-Isbister, "Who Was 'Britain's Most Famous Witch' Sybil Leek?" *Metro*, accessed May 20, 2024, https://metro.co.uk/2024/05/20/britains-famous-witch-sybil-leek-20873623.

a universal mind, a supreme being, from which all forces of life come from, and, through the process of reincarnation, all forces go back."[4] She also referred to herself as a Druid, saying that "witches are the working class, Druids are priests."[5]

Her father taught her about nature, animals, herbs, and Eastern philosophies. Her Russian grandmother taught her witchcraft, astrology, psychic arts, and divination. Authors such as H. G. Wells and Aleister Crowley visited her home often. She wrote about many occult, mystical, and supernatural subjects, covering everything from astrology to working with spirits, herbalism, and even antiques. She owned several antique stores but refused to sell objects related to witchcraft. Leek proposed six tenets of witchcraft: balance, harmony, trust, humility, tolerance, and knowledge. While not universal, these tenets, or tenets very like them, are still used today.

Called eccentric, volatile, and brilliant, Leek had a familiar named Mr. Hotfoot Jackson. He was a jackdaw (a bird in the raven family) who stayed perched on her

4. WFMT Radio (Chicago), "Sybil Leek Discusses Witchcraft and Her Book 'The Jackdaw and the Witch: A True Fable,'" Studs Terkel Radio Archive, 1966, accessed May 20, 2024, https://studsterkel.wfmt.com/programs/sybil-leek-discusses-witchcraft-and-her-book-jackdaw-and-witch-true-fable.
5. Waggoner, "Sybil Leek."

shoulder almost everywhere she went. As a young woman, her Russian grandmother sent her to Gorge du Loup, a town near Nice, France, where Leek replaced a distant relative as the coven's High Priestess. She lived with a group of Romany for a year; they taught her about the forest, herbalism, and ancient folklore. She was known to attend the rituals of Horsa coven, which claimed to be seven hundred years old. She was High Priestess for a short time there.

Given her popularity, she was often pestered by news reporters and tourists. It got to the point that she had to create decoys to distract people to go to secret coven meetings. While in New York, she was contacted by Hans Holzer, a parapsychologist. They did numerous appearances on radio and television. After that, she moved to Los Angeles and met Dr. Israel Regardie, Aleister Crowley's former secretary. They discussed the Qabalah and ritual magic and together performed Golden Dawn rituals.

She was known to be difficult and often argumentative with other witches. She was against nudity in rituals. She did believe in cursing, as opposed to the commonly held "do no harm" position. She was one of the first witches to take on environmental issues, an attitude that became commonplace in the modern era.

Sybil Leek died of cancer in 1982.

A Sampling of Pisces Occultists

LAURIE CABOT

founder of Cabot Tradition of Witchcraft

(March 6, 1933)

KERR CUHULAIN

Canadian Wiccan author and

retired Detective Constable

(March 6, 1954)

CASSANDRA EASON

author of more than 130 books on magick

(March 8, 1948)

MOINA MATHERS

key member of the Hermetic

Order of the Golden Dawn

(February 28, 1965)

BRAD STEIGER

author of books on the paranormal and spirituality

(February 19, 1936)

THE SWAY OF YOUR MOON SIGN

Ivo Dominguez, Jr.

T he Moon is the reservoir of your emotions, thoughts, and all your experiences. The Moon guides your subconscious, your unconscious, and your instinctive response in the moment. The Moon serves as the author, narrator, and the musical score in the ongoing movie in your mind that summarizes and mythologizes your story. The Moon is like a scrying mirror, a sacred well, that gives answers to the question of the meaning of your life. The style and the perspective of your Moon sign shapes your story, a story that starts as a reflection of your Sun sign's impetus. The remembrance of your life events is a condensed subjective story, and it is your Moon sign that summarizes and categorizes the data stream of your life.

In witchcraft, the Moon is our connection and guide to the physical and energetic tides in nature, the astral plane, and other realities. The Moon in the heavens as it moves through signs and phases also pulls and pushes on your aura. The Moon in your birth chart reveals the intrinsic qualities and patterns in your aura, which affect the form your magick takes. Your Sun sign may be the source of your essence and power, but your Moon sign shows how you use that power in your magick. This chapter describes the twelve possible arrangements of Moon signs with a Virgo Sun and what each combination yields.

♈

Moon in Aries

When water and fire mix you get steam, and even more so because this is the last sign and the first sign coming together. This gives you greater drive and intensity than most Pisces and you will rarely get stuck in your life for long. You are courageous, intuitive, and persuasive. When you are going full speed and you are not at your best, you can roll right over people and then regret the pain you've caused later. You are more self-assured and aggressive than most Pisces and are quick to make judgments and conclusions about just about everything. You are warm and caring but will also argue your position with anyone regardless of their status.

You have many talents and interests and a quick mind, but you tend to jump from task to task and miss important details. Success in life will come as you learn to be more focused and learn to plan rather than flying by the seat of your pants. You need a constant stream of new experiences to feel fully alive; don't fight your inclinations, just learn to accept that there is also a need to keep up with mundane tasks. You are adventurous and charming so you will never lack for people to join you in your escapades and exploits. You can be moody at times as you shift between fire and water. Surround yourself with people who are as considerate and honorable as you are so you'll find the right expression of your sensitivity and ambition. You don't mind having a fling, but in general superficial relationships don't interest you.

An Aries Moon, like all the fire element Moons, easily stretches forth to connect with the energy of other beings. These fiery qualities help cleanse and protect your aura from picking up other people's emotional debris or being influenced by your environment. However, your Pisces Sun loves to merge with everything, so intentional cleansing practices are needed. When you draw in power, more will become available, and you rarely run out. This is a gift of your Aries Moon. You do need to be mindful of your flow and to moderate it so that you don't run too hot. The energy field and magick of an Aries Moon tends to move and change faster than any other sign, but it is harder to hold to a specific task or shape. This can be overcome with self-awareness and practice.

Moon in Taurus

A Taurus Moon looks for omens, signs, messages, and synchronicities around you to give you guidance. The universe is always speaking to you. This combination tends to accentuate your Pisces gifts but makes them more grounded and keeps you clearheaded. This earthy sign also makes you more concerned about money and practical concerns. You have good people skills and know how to work with others and bring out the best in them. You are loyal and caring and have a long fuse, but when you've hit your limit, you can transform into an implacable bull. You are good at hiding your emotional scars. This is mostly a good thing, but it also means you must choose to let people know when they've transgressed and hurt your feelings. If you don't sooner or later, you'll snap at someone and then regret it.

This combination usually gives deep emotions, a sensual nature, a romantic heart, and a need for physical reassurance. Your energy is very attractive, so it will draw people to you whether or not you are trying. In your relationships and friendships, you need stability and a sense of sanctuary. If that is not present, then it may be best to move on. Try to let go of harsh feelings and grudges as they are a waste of your precious time. The Taurus Moon also gives you a knack for understanding how to use different mediums for creating art or music. Learn to trust your creative urges and just let yourself get into the zone and let it flow. One of the downsides to a Pisces-Taurus energy is that you are more prone to getting lost in your desires and obsessions of the moment and overindulging.

A Taurus Moon generates an aura that is magnetic and pulls energy inward. This magnetic tendency is amplified by your Pisces Sun. You are good at collecting and concentrating energy for yourself for magickal purposes. This Moon also makes it easier to create strong shields and defenses. If something does manage to breach your protection or create some other type of energetic injury, get some healing help. Generally, people with a Taurus Moon have less flexibility in their aura, but this is moderated by the water of your Sun. You can work toward improving your flexibility by leaning into the power of water. Shape-shifting and soul travel in the form of an animal may be one of your gifts. Seashells and sea glass make good focal points for your power.

Ⅱ

Moon in Gemini

This is a volatile and highly changeable combination with Gemini's mutability stirring up Pisces's mutable water. All your senses, physical and psychic, tend to be wide open all the time. This lets you notice things that are missed by others. This makes you a poet and a visionary and a conduit for spiritual messages. You are a quick learner, which is a good thing because you want to try a bit of everything. Your thought process is quick, quirky, and brilliant, but you may have some difficulties in communicating them effectively to others. Try to slow down and divide up your ideas into manageable chunks when speaking or writing. You are adaptable, inventive, and can brainstorm dozens of ideas in moments. The most common challenge with this combination is that it is hard to make a choice and to stick with it. You see more possibilities than there is time to accomplish them. This is only true when you forget to prioritize things, so make a list and put reminders in your calendar.

You are good at rationalizing things to manage discomforts, but some type of meditation or relaxation process would be helpful. You are tolerant, open-minded, and compassionate, but don't forget to think about yourself and your needs. The people who feed your soul are communicative and understanding of the full range of your deep emotions. You are excellent as a listener, so professions that make use of this talent will be the most rewarding. You have a gift for cheering people up and reminding them of the good things in life, especially in difficult times.

A Gemini Moon, like all the air Moons, makes it easier to engage in psychism and gives the aura greater flexibility. You have a quicksilver aura that seeks connection but not a merger with other beings and energies. When an air type aura reaches out and touches something, it can quickly read and copy the patterns that it finds. A Gemini Moon gives the capacity to quickly adapt and respond to changing energy conditions in working magick or using the psychic senses. However, turbulent spiritual atmospheres are felt strongly and can be uncomfortable or cause harm. A wind can pick up and carry dust and debris and the same is true for an aura. If you need to cleanse your energy, become still, and the debris will simply fall out of your aura.

Moon in Cancer

Double water greatly increases your Piscean sensitivity, empathy, and insight. This makes you very aware of people's emotions, and the Cancer Moon strengthens your desire to help them. This can also be generalized to groups or society so you may become involved in nonprofit and humanitarian efforts. You may be called to become a healer and a helper in matters of physical health, mental health, or society. Be careful because you can be easily hurt by those you try to help. Remind yourself that this is more about the situation than you as an individual. This combination isn't usually attracted to leadership positions, but it is common to find yourself falling into those roles as if it were fated. You are likely to be shy and prefer to be a homebody, but it is important to develop strategies to be more present and active in the broader world. It is important that you have the solitude you need to recharge so that you can do the things you are called to do.

Both Pisces and Cancer have a strong self-protective urge. How much this governs your life depends on whether you build a fortress of trust in your capacity to heal yourself. Also create a place within yourself that is filled with the sure knowledge of your worth as an individual. The people you choose to be your family of choice need to be aware of your true nature and affirm all that you are. Even constructive criticism is hard for you, so pick people who are consistently supportive. Also, unsolicited advice is often unwanted and unhelpful. It is a warning sign that you need self-care when you can't find time for your spiritual pursuits.

A Cancer Moon, like all the water Moons, gives the aura a magnetic pull that wants to merge with whatever is nearby. Imagine two drops of water growing closer until they barely touch and how they pull together to become one larger drop. The aura of a person with a Cancer Moon is more likely to retain the patterns and energies that it touches. This can be a good thing or a problem depending on what is absorbed. You must take extra care to cleanse and purify yourself before and after magickal work whenever possible. One of the gifts that comes with this Moon is a capacity for healing that offers comfort while filling in and healing disruptions in other people's energy. Divination, divine embodiment, and devotional rituals are your core as a witch.

♌

Moon in Leo

This Moon makes you flamboyant, more enthusiastic, and bolder than other Pisceans on the surface. The emotional power or water and the passion and purpose of fire make you formidable, and you always attract attention with your charm and open heart. You have the capacity to lift people up or to drag them down. Make sure that the prodigious force of this combination is used in a way that matches your ideals and your goals. There is some conflict between your Pisces Sun's desire for peace and your Leo Moon's desire to make a big splash and maybe conquer the world. Both your Sun and Moon agree that your personal honor and beliefs must be maintained and upheld. There is always a heroic or big picture subtext to all you do.

Your actions often put you center stage or in the front as the vanguard. When you worry that you may enjoy the attention too much, ask yourself who or what you are working for. Don't worry, you are probably taking on those roles for all the right reasons.

Acts of service for people or for causes recharge your batteries. If you see something that needs to be done, you will do it without waiting for permission. Take time to enjoy the pleasures of life but with moderation as excess is built into this combination. You can be dramatic, so when you bring new people into your life, ease them in slowly. It can be startling when you move from one persona to another to become what is needed in that moment. You are bighearted and a considerate friend or lover. Don't assume everyone has good intentions; take off the rose-colored glasses periodically.

A Leo Moon, like all the fire element Moons, easily stretches forth to connect with the energy of other beings. The fiery qualities act to cleanse and protect your aura from picking up other people's emotional debris or being influenced by your environment. The Leo Moon also makes it easier for you to find your center and stay centered. The fixed fire of Leo makes it easier to hold large amounts of energy that can be applied for individual and collective workings. You are particularly well suited to ritual leadership or at the role of being the primary shaper of energy in a working. Combined with your Pisces Sun, this Moon is good leading or creating rituals, summoning spirits, and cleansing people or places of negative energy.

♍

Moon in Virgo

This is the rare Pisces that is equally aware of the details of the physical world and the subtle world of energy, spirits, and consciousness. You have the gifts of rational analysis and intuition. Many people will think that you are shy, but the truth is that you move with care, subtlety, and purpose in most settings. You study and ponder people, feelings, nature, and society; your happiness and fulfillment depend on how you categorize and organize your findings. The story that you tell yourself becomes your experience of day-to-day life. Also, the more you encourage others to think and examine their own lives, the more you will feel like you are following one of your life's purposes. You are a good organizer, but you'll be more content if you are not the boss and let someone else take the heat.

Ethics and doing your best are important to you and this is admirable. Try not to judge yourself harshly when you miss the mark or make a mistake. Everyone knows that you are conscientious and will pardon any lapse. You are also generous and forgiving of other people's mistakes, but if you detect meanness and spite, you will not give that person an iota of respect. Get all the facts before coming to a conclusion because sometimes you overreact. The people you turn to for guidance and support need to be modest and down to earth. Even though you have an earth Moon, you need people who can keep you grounded. You are a perfectionist and prefer calm environments, so take your time in selecting friends and partners. Meditation, handcrafts, and time in nature are the best medicine for you. At several points in your life, you will need to look at your childhood and younger years and reframe their meaning. This is vital work that must not be avoided.

A Virgo Moon, like all the earth element Moons, generates an aura that is magnetic and pulls energy inward. This Moon also makes it easier to create strong thoughtforms and energy constructs. Virgo Moons are best at perceiving and understanding patterns and process in auras, energy, spells, and so on. You can be quite good at spotting what is off and finding a way to remedy the situation. This gives the potential to do healing work and curse breaking among other things. The mixture of Virgo Moon with Pisces Sun makes it easier to organize spells and rituals. You are likely to be good at creating oils, potions, and incense blends.

♎

Moon in Libra

The dual nature of Libra and Pisces brings the conscious mind and the subconscious into a balance that allows an easy exchange between the two. When you relax and go with the flow, brilliant ideas will come pouring forth from your lips. More than most Pisces, you have a strong drive to explore occultism and metaphysics. You have talent for finding beauty in almost anything, and that brings you joy that you can share with others. Although you can enjoy the simple things, you have refined tastes that draw you to the most expensive options. You are more sociable than most Pisces and probably have a large number of associates and friends. You do your best to offer kindness and fairness to everyone. In your conversations and negotiations with people, you are an expert at winning minds through hearts. You understand how emotions shape most of the actions in the world.

When you do run into difficulties and find that you are stuck, you'll only dig yourself in deeper if you try to rationalize the situation. Don't forget your psychic gifts will often give you the missing clues. Harmony and balance are the touchstones in your life. If you find that you are becoming stubborn or dramatic, it means that you need to change your course or your tactics. Flexibility is one of your greatest strengths. It is easy for you to get motivated if you are helping people, but you have a harder time staying determined when it comes to your own work. The people who bring you joy tend to be playful, creative, and hopeful. Keep the proportions equal between the people who support you and the people you help out of duty or you'll be exhausted.

A Libra Moon, like all the air Moons, makes it easier to engage in soul travel and psychism and gives the aura greater flexibility. When you are working well with your Libra Moon, you can make yourself a neutral and clear channel for information from spirits and other entities. You are also able to tune in to unspoken requests when doing divinatory work. The auras of people with Libra Moon are very capable at bridging and equalizing differences between the subtle bodies of groups of people. This allows you to bring order and harmony to energies raised and shaped in a group ritual. You may have a talent for bargaining with spirits and creating beautiful altars, magickal objects, and spells.

♏

Moon in Scorpio

It's all or nothing with this combination because this Moon amplifies rather than moderates your Pisces characteristics. Whether it is work, relationships, love, or hate, you will be all in and intense. You are absolutely the best in times of crisis when you become focused and cannot be swayed from accomplishing whatever needs to be done. You are intensely curious and inquisitive and will ferret out every detail and secret when you choose to learn or examine something. Your powers of observation are strong, and your memory is long. Be cautious when offering criticism as your insights are often sharper than you think and can cut deeply. You are better than most Pisces at masking your emotions. Most people are not mind readers, so drop some clues if you want to be understood.

You have an astounding amount of creative energy inside you. You could be an artist, a writer, a politician, an event organizer, a religious leader, an infamous celebrity, or almost anything. It is a matter of passion, imagination, and follow-through, and you can do it. Oddly, your life is more stable and comfortable when you have enough projects to work on. If you aren't active enough, your life stalls out. The scale of your life is also yours to decide. You crave a primal and deep closeness with a select few you let into your heart. For you, intimacy is both spiritual and sensual and your partners must understand this for you to be happy. True candor and honesty are your baseline expectations for all the people in your life.

A Scorpio Moon, like all the water Moons, gives the aura a magnetic pull that wants to merge with whatever is nearby. You easily absorb information about other people, spirits, places, and so on. The energy and magick of a Scorpio Moon is adept at probing and moving past barriers, shields, and wards. This also gives you the power to remove things that should not be present in healing work. This combination also makes it easier for you to imbue objects with power, spell work, or consecrations. You may have a gift for hypnosis or guiding people into trance. Opening portals is a natural gift that would serve you better with some training for control. You can be very good at divine possession and oracular work, but you need people to ward you and watch over you to keep you safe.

Moon in Sagittarius

This Moon gives you an abundance of zeal, optimism, and the energy to pursue your dreams and interests. You are outspoken and have a hard time bottling up your thoughts or feelings. You are daring, curious, and love travel and if for some reason you can't travel, you do so with your mind. This combination tends to produce a strong fascination with spirituality, religion, the occult, and deeper philosophical pursuits. You are friendly, fun loving, and consistently kind to others. When you are excited about something, you revel in sharing your enthusiasm with others. The more complicated things in life are open books to you, and the simple and practical is shrouded in mystery. You don't look for conflict, but you are prone to blurting out the truth as you see it without taking a beat to consider the consequences. While most Pisces prefer to be conciliatory and endeavor to avoid conflict, you are more inclined to jump in and start a debate.

There are two character flaws that you must guard against. You tend to jump to conclusions before you have enough information. You also love imagining and brainstorming, but creating a detailed plan and implementing it don't seem exciting to you. You tend to be happier with friends and loved ones who give you space when needed and help you with the more real-world details of life. You are more resilient than most Pisces and will recover quickly from hardships. The accumulation of adverse experiences just makes you more empathetic to other people's struggles. You do have a need for freedom and a desire to explore new territories so you may settle down later in life or have many relationships.

The auras of people with Sagittarius Moon are the most adaptable of the fire Moons. Your energy can reach far and change its shape easily. You are particularly good at affecting other people's energy or the energy of a place. Like the other fire Moons, your aura is good at cleansing itself, but it is not automatic and requires your conscious choice. The mutable fire of Sagittarius is changeable and can go from a small ember to a pillar of fire that reaches the sky. It is important that you manage your energy, so it is somewhere between the extremes of almost out and furious inferno. This aura has star power when you light it up, and physical and nonphysical beings will look and listen. You also have a gift for facilitating the process of calling and integrating all the parts of your psyche.

♑

Moon in Capricorn

The cardinal earth of this Moon gives you a strong personality with more drive, common sense, and ambition than other Pisces. You can be warmhearted and kind, but you never lose track of whether or not you are looking after yourself. Your feelings are powerful and complicated when it comes to personal matters. You are compassionate, stoic when needed, and have a strong work ethic. You have the greatest clarity when you are thinking about your work and projects. You have great reserves of energy, intellect, and intuition. You are judicious in your use of intellect and psychism. Even when engaged in mundane tasks, you do not lose sight. The downside to this combination is that you can be too serious, pessimistic, and may wallow in your few failings. The longer you stay in that state of mind the more likely you are to create trouble for yourself and others.

You don't need a partner, but you generally want one until you learn to love yourself. When you are in a relationship, you are passionate, protective, and attentive. The same is true with the small group of people you count as friends. You are a pillar of strength for both friends and your community. You are very independent and hold to your own goals and directions, but you keep track of what is going in on the lives of the people you care about. If there is a crisis, you will swoop in and do what you can to help. You view this assistance as a matter of honor and reciprocity. While you wish to continually improve yourself, come to terms with the fact that you do have plateaus and limits. You see the world too clearly, which may make you cynical, but this is something you must shake off. Don't forget to use your wonderfully wicked sense of humor.

A Capricorn Moon generates an aura that is magnetic and pulls energy inward. What you draw to yourself tends to stick and solidify, so be wary, especially when doing healing work or cleansings. The magick of a Capricorn Moon is excellent at imposing a pattern or creating a container in a working. Your spells and workings tend to be durable. You also have a knack for building wards and doing protective magick. You have a gift for manifesting the seemingly impossible. You have a gift for creating traditions and practices that can be used by many. Road opening and uncrossing work comes easily to you.

Moon in Aquarius

This combination brings together two different streams of humanitarian urges. Both share idealistic views of the future with Aquarius focused on systems and Pisces on spiritual unity. Since we are in the churn of moving from the Age of Pisces to the Age of Aquarius, your life will connect to the work of the transition. You have a wide range of friends and associates from many walks of life. You can read people's reactions quickly and adjust your words and body language on the fly. Sometimes you don't realize that you are unconventional, cutting edge, avant-garde, and that most of the people around you live in the past, not even the present. Your desire to share your views and ideas is very strong, but be careful that you don't push so hard that you push people away. Let your Pisces Sun rule your actions when dealing with people.

Your farsighted attitude makes you a bit of a rebel. You will be tempted to take on the world by yourself, but it is better if you recruit some help. Your rebellious nature also makes you sensitive, perhaps overly sensitive, to anything that feels confining or pokes at your pride. Stay flexible and wriggle out of conflicts. Wait until you can pick the time and place for difficult conversations. The persona the world sees is mysterious and unpredictable. Thankfully you give off an innocent and divine energy that tells the world that your intentions come from a place of caring. You are especially good at pointing out the silver lining or the first rays of dawn when times are stormy or dark. Make sure that you have people in your life who will give you a safe and caring space to be yourself and let down your public persona.

Like all the air Moons, the Aquarius Moon encourages a highly mobile and flexible aura. This Moon works best when it is focused by the enveloping emotion of your Pisces Sun. Grounding is important, but focusing on your core and center is more important. In this case, it is your heart center you can strengthen to stabilize your power. People with Aquarius Moon are good at shaping and holding a specific thoughtform or energy pattern and transferring it to other people or into objects. You are good at casting spells spontaneously with just a few minutes to focus. You have a gift for revealing or augmenting other people's psychic and magickal talents.

♓

Moon in Pisces

Being a double Pisces sign, mutable water can express itself in many ways. You may alternate between feeling connected to everyone and everything. Then it may be too much, and you retreat into your inner world and take refuge in your imagination. It is essential that you learn to manage this connection, empathy, so that it becomes your greatest tool rather than a burden. Listen to your deep wisdom and guidance as to when to open up and when to shield. Make your home environment as comfortable and appealing so that it can be your sanctuary. It is your nature to be at peace and feel that you have a purpose; when you don't, you are probably picking up on external forces. Pay close attention to your dreams, daydreams, and visions as they are how you process your deepest thoughts and longings.

The arts can be the core of your work in the world and how you communicate the most effectively. Use that profound and brilliant imagination to envision a better world; that's how it begins. The people around you will eventually understand you, but give them time to experience all your sides and facets. Be patient and wait for the tide to turn and your time will come. Your physical health also relies on keeping yourself in equilibrium. In matters of the heart, you are very giving, and when you love someone, you overlook their flaws. You are a romantic; embrace it and you'll be happier. For some, this will be actual courtship, and for others, it will be the romance of taking on an eccentric role, such as the mystic, the witch people turn to, or the keeper of wonder who reveals the mystery of existence to others.

With a Pisces Moon, the emphasis should be on learning to feel and control the rhythm of the energetic motion of your aura. Water Moon sign auras are flexible, cohesive, and magnetic, so they tend to ripple and rock like the action of waves. Pisces Moon is the most likely to pick up and hang on to unwanted emotions or energies. Be careful; develop good cleansing practices for yourself, your workplace, and your home. Pisces Moon people are the best at energizing, comforting, and healing disruptions in other people's auras. You are also good at casting illusions, glamours, spells of stealth, and obscuration. Your double Pisces energy lets you use this Moon to find the best possible futures out of the many possibilities in divination or to restore the flow of power where it has been blocked.

TAROT
CORRESPONDENCES

You can use the tarot cards in your work as a Pisces witch for more than divination. They can be used as focal points in meditations and trance to connect with the power of your sign or element or to understand them more fully. They are great on your altar as an anchor for the powers you are calling. You can use the Minor Arcana cards to tap into Saturn, Jupiter, or Mars in Pisces energy even when they are in other signs in the heavens. If you take a picture of a card, shrink the image and print it out; you can fold it up and place it in spell bags or jars as an ingredient.

Pisces Major Arcana

The Moon

All the Water Signs

The Ace of Cups

Pisces Minor Arcana

8 of Cups	Saturn in Pisces
9 of Cups	Jupiter in Pisces
10 of Cups	Mars in Pisces

Mat Auryn

I think my most Pisces witch moment involves another witch I know, one of my witchcraft teachers Laurie Cabot, whose birthday is the day after mine. Laurie helped bring the importance of psychic ability back into witchcraft with her book *Power of the Witch* and her classes. She was also featured on many television shows because of her extraordinary psychic ability. The experience occurred when I took her classes for the first degree in the Cabot Tradition of Witchcraft. One of the exercises we had to do on this specific night was to meet our spirit guide. Laurie led us on a trance meditation where we would contact this spirit and share the experience afterward with the class.

I must give a little background before I continue this story. Before this night, I already had a strong relationship with a spirit who often takes the form of a barn owl but has shown me time and again that she isn't a barn owl spirit; it's just a form she often takes when interacting with me. I wrote about this owl in my book *Psychic Witch* when discussing synchronicity. I share how after my first contact with her, I saw owls everywhere the next day in various forms, to the point that it was undeniably a sign that the experience was not just a fantasy or delusion, but something was behind it. I also requested that Llewellyn put a barn owl on the cover in honor of this spirit so dear to me. It's essential for me also to point out that this class was before I had even signed a contract for *Psychic Witch*, and no one knew about my connection with this spirit, as I kept it private.

However, whenever I'm learning from another teacher or in a specific tradition or occult order, I always try to enter with a beginner's mind. I try not to carry any projections of past experiences or expectations into what I'm learning or engaging in for the duration of that training or magickal work. I do this to be open to new experiences and perspectives that I might not otherwise experience if I didn't have that beginner's attitude. So even before we began the guided meditation, I had already set aside my expectations of seeing that spirit that often takes on the guise of a barn owl. I was expecting to experience someone in human form but wasn't sure what that spirit might look like or how our interaction would go.

My spirit, who takes the form of a barn owl, will often perch on my shoulder in my mind's eye, and there have been rare occasions where she's even been photographed by accident, appearing as a slight owl-sized blur of light on the shoulder she often sits on. During this night, I felt her on my shoulder as I often do. That was until I closed my eyes to enter the alpha brainwave state under Laurie's guided instructions. As soon as I entered the alpha brainwave state, I no longer felt her on my physical shoulder. I figured it must be because I was meeting a new and different spirit guide, and she didn't want to interfere with the experience, which is also what I wanted.

After the alpha brainwave state induction, Laurie began guiding our meditation. To my surprise, as my inner vision began to take over, that spirit, who often takes the form of a barn owl, was on the shoulder of my inner plane's vision of myself. Slightly annoyed that I felt like I was projecting something into the experience, I did my best to ignore the spirit and focus with all my might on Laurie's instructions. But here was that little owl annoyingly on the shoulder of my inner self during the entirety of the guided meditation. I'm not sure I'm allowed to give specifics of what that particular trance meditation consisted of, but it's safe to say that there's a point where you meet the spirit guide, as that's the entire purpose of that exercise. When it came to the part where we met our spirit guide, the little owl humorously and, to my irritation, just flew from my shoulder to the spot where our spirit guide was supposed to be located. It's almost as if she was saying, "Oh, is it time now? I guess I'll just fly over there if that's what you really want." So I sat with this experience in the meditation, and my spirit informed me that she was the same spirit I was supposed to seek in this experience and that she and I didn't just have contact, but we had already forged a strong bond.

When the meditation was over, and as my other classmates and I were grounding ourselves back into physical reality, Laurie asked us to share our experiences individually. She was sitting at the front of the classroom behind her desk. The rest of us were lined up in rows of chairs facing her desk. One by one, people began to share their experiences about the spirit people they met. My little owl had returned to my physical shoulder, perching as she often does. I sat listening to the experiences of those around me, getting a bit insecure as they each discussed the type of spirit people they had met and shared messages they had given them. Then it was my turn.

I cleared my throat and gently said, "Well, the spirit I saw was an owl."

"A what?" Laurie asked, making sure she heard me correctly.

"An owl..." I repeated.

Then Laurie simply replied, "No. We aren't doing animal spirits right now. We're doing a different type of spirit guide. So you'll have to retry the exercise again later."

Laurie moved on to the next person, who began sharing their experience. Feeling slightly embarrassed but more upset that I messed up something that should have been so easy for me as a Pisces who excels at those inner visionary experiences, I brought my attention to my shoulder and the spirit sitting there. I was unsure who was correct in this situation. So I asked my spirit to give me a clear sign that it was the spirit I was meant to "find" on my journey. Almost immediately, the spirit vanished. Crap! Had I just gotten lost in my imagination and fantasy? After everyone had finished their experiences, Laurie continued the class. The whole time, I was trying not to be disappointed with myself or embarrassed.

At the end of the class, Laurie called me to her desk while everyone was getting up and ready to leave. I approached the desk, assuming she would reaffirm that I had to do the exercise again. Instead, as soon as the class was clear of everyone except for a few Cabot priests and priestesses assisting the class as teacher's aides for Laurie, she began to speak.

"That owl," Laurie began. I could feel my embarrassment and humility swelling inside me again. Surely she will tell me that I did it wrong and need to do it again.

"Is the owl a little white owl, like a barn owl?" she inquired, peering at me through her large black-rimmed glasses.

"Yes," I answered with humility.

"But she's not *really* a barn owl, is she? You already know this little owl, and she sometimes appears differently."

I was surprised at this question and even more surprised she gendered the spirit as female, as most of my peers in my class had guides that matched their genders.

"No, she's not. It's just a form she likes to take with me often for some reason."

"That's what I thought. Let me tell you something. After you spoke and I went on to the next person to share their experience, this little white owl flew right up to me from your direction and was persistent in getting my attention. I had trouble focusing on what the other people were trying to share because she was so distracting. But she made it clear to me that she wasn't an owl spirit. So I don't think you need to repeat that exercise. When you said an owl, I had assumed it was an owl spirit, but she clarified that she isn't."

This was the confirmation I was looking for! Laurie, a Pisces and a world-renowned Psychic witch affirmed the owl and got specifics. She knew the species of owl, her gender, and that I already had a relationship with this owl. Laurie also knew that it wasn't an owl in the sense of an animal spirit, but rather it was more of a form that the spirit liked to take. Most of all, she flew up to Laurie exactly when I had perceived she had disappeared from my shoulder. As I left the building for the night to return home, I sensed that little owl back on my shoulder with a renewed and heightened trust in my psychic and visionary abilities.

Between Earth and Starry Heaven Pisces Exercise

Thea Sabin

Some astrologers say, Pisces, that the story of humankind is told in the twelve astrological signs. It begins when bold Aries wills us into being by proclaiming "I am!" and it culminates when Pisces partly untethers from the material earth and stretches toward the heavens, declaring, "I *believe*." Pisces's symbol is two fish swimming in opposite directions, connected by a wispy cord between their mouths. One fish is the earthly realm, and the other is the spiritual. It makes perfect sense that Pisces rules the feet in medical astrology, because Pisceans are moving their metaphorical feet between those worlds constantly.

Pisceans get picked on for being absent-minded. Not present. Daydreamers. But what others don't realize is one of Pisces's greatest strengths—the ability to blurt out a startlingly relevant insight, apparently from nowhere—is born from the intuitive knowledge gained during their mental walkabouts. Pisceans do tend to favor the spiritual heavens fish over the earthly one, and learning to come back down to the ground and be present when they'd rather be swimming through the stars can make a Pisces witch even more powerful. Here's a basic mindfulness trick to help.

You will need:

- ⬦ A smooth, pocket-sized energy-absorbing rock (river rock, obsidian, jet, or hematite)
- ⬦ A quiet place where you can be alone for about thirty minutes

Instructions:

Start by sitting comfortably in a chair with your feet flat on the floor. Take three slow, deep breaths. Pick up the rock. Feel how solid it is. Notice its shape and how it feels against your skin. Say,

> *I am a child of earth. When I hold this rock, I'm fully present.*

Rub your thumb across the rock. Breathe. Focus your attention on your Pisces feet. Feel how they connect solidly to the floor. See or feel or imagine them connecting to the earth below it. Say,

> *I'm secure, grounded, and present.*

Breathe. Rub the rock. See or feel or imagine a line of energy between the rock, your feet, and the earth. Say,

> *I'm connected and aware of my surroundings.*

Rub the rock again. Breathe. Know that whenever you hold this rock, you can bring yourself to the present, focus, ground, or connect to earth. See or feel or imagine your connection to the earth through the rock and your feet. Rub the rock. Say,

> *I am a child of earth and starry heaven, and I choose which realm I inhabit and when.*

Breathe. Use your senses to notice things in the room. What do you see? Hear? Smell? Take time to be present. If you find your mind drifting off, acknowledge that without judgment, rub the rock, and notice things in the room again.

Repeat the exercise until the phrase "I am a child of earth" and the rock become triggers for centering yourself in the here and now. Eventually you won't need the triggers.

YOUR RISING SIGN'S INFLUENCE

Ivo Dominguez, Jr.

The rising sign, also known as the ascendant, is the sign that was rising on the eastern horizon at the time and place of your birth. In the birth chart, it is on the left side on the horizontal line that divides the upper and lower halves of the chart. Your rising sign is also the cusp of your first house. It is often said that the rising sign is the mask that you wear to the world, but it is much more than that. It is also the portal through which you experience the world. The sign of your ascendant colors and filters those experiences. Additionally, when people first meet you, they meet your rising sign. This means that they interact with you based on their perception of that sign rather than your Sun sign. This in turn has an impact on you and how you view yourself. As they get to know you over time, they'll meet you as your Sun sign. Your ascendant is like the colorful clouds that hide the Sun at dawn, and as the Sun continues to rise, it is revealed.

The rising sign will also have an influence on your physical appearance as well as your style of dress. To some degree your voice, mannerisms, facial expressions, stance, and gait are also swayed by the sign of your ascendant. The building blocks of your public persona come from your rising sign. How you arrange those building blocks is guided by your Sun sign, but your Sun sign must work with what it has been given. For witches, the rising sign shows some of the qualities and foundations for the magickal personality you can construct. The magickal personality is much more than simply the shifting into the right headspace, collecting ritual gear, the lighting of candles, and so on. The magickal persona is a construct that is developed through your magickal and spiritual practices to serve as an interface between different parts of the self. The magickal persona, also known as the magickal personality, can also act as a container or boundary so that the mundane and the magickal parts of a person's life can each have its own space. Your rising also gives clues about which magickal techniques will come naturally to you.

This chapter describes the twelve possible arrangements of rising signs with a Pisces Sun and what each combination produces. There are 144 possible kinds of Pisces when you take into consideration the Moon signs and rising signs. You may wish to reread the chapter on your Moon sign after reading about your rising sign so you can better understand these influences when they are merged.

♈ Aries Rising

You are seen as more confident and assertive than most Pisces. You boldly take your Piscean dreams and try to make them realities. You also seek out challenges to test yourself and to feel more alive. You have a strong sense of purpose. This combination is more fitness focused and physically active than most Pisces. Be cautious that you don't overindulge in life's physical pleasures because you are drawn to excess, especially substances. You can also come across as too forceful and impetuous, so take care that you don't create pointless drama. Take it down a notch or you'll be frustrated by the outcomes.

You secretly enjoy conflict, but be aware that other approaches may serve you better.

This combination makes you quick, decisive, incisive, and you radiate a vitality that attracts others. You love to get things done quickly but slow down enough to use your intuition. Your friends and partners need to be resilient and energetic to keep up with you. Take some time to think before jumping into new friendships or relationships. You tend to go until you drop. Try to live as if you have all the time in the world. Time is flexible when viewed through the eyes of a Pisces witch. Physical activity is important to maintain your physical health and to blow off steam.

An Aries rising means that when you reach out to draw in power, fire will answer faster and more intensely. Use your Pisces water to shape that power. This combination makes it easier for you to summon and call forth spirits and powers and create bindings. The creation of servitors, amulets, and charms is favored as well. This rising amplifies all types of magick for yourself and others. You can sense trouble long before it is evident to others and come up with countermeasures quickly.

☉

Taurus Rising

A Taurus rising brings geniality and openness that complements Pisces's empathetic nature. This combination gives you more firmness of personality to hold your own when your opinions are opposed. You seem easygoing and placid on the outside, but your internal world is still very changeable, and you feel pulled in many directions. You have greater stamina for work and details than most Pisces once you get going. One of your challenges is breaking the inertia to begin your tasks. Taurus loves safety and Pisces revels in feeling connected and included, so home and hearth are very important to you.

It is easier for you to talk about other people's emotions, but you are shy when it comes to expressing yours. You are extremely loyal and loving, but don't expect your friends or partners to match you in this regard. People show love, affection, and loyalty in different ways. Be on guard against becoming too possessive or protective of the people you care about. As you get older, try to maintain or increase your level of physical activity to lift up your vitality and to keep your body comfortable. You may tend to avoid seeking healthcare. It is better to attend to matters when they are small, so they don't become serious.

Taurus rising strengthens your aura and the capacity to maintain a more solid shape to your energy. This gives you stronger shields and allows you to create thoughtforms and spells that are longer lasting. This combination makes it a bit harder to call energy, but once it is started, the flow is strong. You have a powerful gift for invocations, trance work, and hypnosis. This combo also makes it easier to work with nature spirits, animal spirits, and plants. You have a knack for spells to reveal the past, what is hidden, or to find your best options for a happy outcome.

♊

Gemini Rising

This rising sharpens your communication skills and makes you a compelling writer, speaker, editor, and fan of many genres. You are more inquisitive about everything and everyone than most Pisces. You move from interest to interest with great energy and must strive to finish one thing before beginning the next. If something is new, you're even more intrigued. You are adventuresome, which means you break rules more frequently than your Pisces Sun finds comfortable. Your self-confidence needs regular boosting, so learn to nurture yourself and listen to supportive friends. Companionship is the essential part of love for you. No matter how exciting the situation, if that is not present, the relationship will not endure.

You come across as bright, charming, and genuinely interested in the people around you. You love to tease and be playful one minute and then dead serious the next. You will have a spark of childlike energy your entire life. You love frequent change in your home, social life, and work and you'll need friends and partners who are comfortable with this. This rising draws you into intellectual pursuits and the promotion of ideas. You are also good at making deals and agreements. You can juggle ideas and imagination so easily that you may lose track of what is real and what is the creation of your wishes or fears.

Gemini rising combines your Pisces intuition to make you skillful at writing spells and rituals that make good use of invocations and symbols. This rising helps your energy and aura stretch farther and to adapt to whatever it touches. You would do well to develop your receptive psychic skills as well as practices such as mediumship and channeling. You may have a gift for interpreting dreams and the words that come from oracles and seers. This combination often has a knack for knowing how best to use music, incense, crystals, and props in magick.

Cancer Rising

The cardinal water and mutable water of your rising and Sun greatly magnify the Pisces gifts and challenges of sensitivity and emotional response. You are romantic, nostalgic, and are drawn to the wistful, the forlorn, and the otherworldly. You are more easily hurt than most Pisces, though you still manage to shine and lift others' spirits. You have an excellent memory and a love of knowledge, especially history and the humanities. You are a devoted friend and lover and adore nesting and creating a unique home. You keep secrets well and are good as a confidante. You want to go with your gut most of the time, but that is not a good idea because your feelings shift too quickly.

It takes time to find the right work and profession, but it will happen. Listen to the advice of the more successful people you know. You need a bit more structure and organization in daily affairs. As the years go by, your life gets better and your status rises. You can be too intense and exhaust your friends and loved ones. Fear of loss can generate loss. Your success in relationships is directly correlated to developing skill at regulating your emotions. Your gut and digestive health is strongly affected by your emotional state; use it as an indicator to attend to your distress.

Cancer grants the power to use your emotions, or the emotional energy of others, to power your witchcraft. Though you can draw on a wide range of energies to fuel your magick, raising power through emotion is the simplest. You have a gift for clairvoyance, scrying, and animal communication. Moon magick for practical workings for abundance or healing of the heart comes easily for you. Color magick such as the choice of colors for candles, altar cloths, robes, banners, and color visualization can also serve you well.

♌

Leo Rising

The fixed strength of this rising can provide light and warmth that bring out the best in your Pisces nature. You have a deep confidence in your ability to do what would be impossible for many others. You constantly strive to manifest success in all its forms. You truly want to make life better for other people and it is one of your life purposes. One of your challenges is that you have many talents and are torn about which ones should be your focus. You have great charisma and have the power to inspire and lead others. Love and dignity should serve as the keywords to guiding the impact you have on the world.

You are a loyal friend, but sometimes the desire to be helpful becomes meddling. In matters of love and friendship, you have powerful appetites and passions that must be fulfilled. Be honest and speak the truth of your needs and boundaries. In personal matters, your hardest lesson is to learn to see people as they are instead of how you wish they would be. Outwardly you look confident, but internally you have many worries and doubts. Be patient as those close to you get to see and understand your inner self. You prefer quality over quantity in most things in life.

Leo rising means that when you reach out to draw in power, fire will answer as easily as water. Focus on the flexibility in your energy and imagination to access the other elements. Your aura and energy are brighter and sturdier than most people, so you attract the attention of spirits, deities, and so on. Whether or not showing up so clearly in the other worlds is a gift or a challenge is up to you. Your Sun and rising give you a knack for healing and transformative work. You do better in rituals and workings with props, incense, candles, and other sensory stimuli.

♍

Virgo Rising

Virgo's earthiness helps you be more practical and detail focused than many Pisces. You are a mix of the analytical and the creative and your vision is wide ranging. You aspire to perfection so hard sometimes that you lose your sense of perspective and context. In your personal life and your work life, be watchful against focusing on the flaws and errors. It is extremely hard for you to ask for favors or accept help that is freely given. This is one of your most serious weaknesses. This may be because you have been taken advantage of in the past. Use your instinct and keen observational skills to separate the gold from fool's gold.

You love your interests and projects as much as, maybe more, than you do people. Do not turn small glitches into major problems; try to maintain a sense of proportion in your relationships. You tend to give too much and not expect enough from others. You'll be happier if you correct this imbalance. Just because you notice and sense a multitude of things does not mean that they are worthy of your attention. Try not to fret so much. When you are stressed out, you can convince yourself that you are sick and eventually manifest illness.

Virgo rising with a Pisces Sun makes it easier to work with goddesses and gods and other powers related to healing, nature, and wisdom. You have a knack for creating connections between different kinds of magick and making them combine. Magickal research, past-life work, bindings, and cord-cutting spells are favored by this combination. Be careful when you entwine your energy with someone else's because you can pick up and retain their patterns and issues. Always cleanse your energy after doing solo or collective work. Adapting old rituals or magickal methods to modern times is one of your talents.

♎

Libra Rising

Your Libra rising makes you appealing, engaging, and persuasive. You feel that part of your work this life is building lasting harmony and understanding. This is how you want to make your mark in the world. You do this by teasing deep issues to the surface with seemingly casual conversation. You know how to bide your time and act at the right moment. You can be very indecisive, so it is better to have a structured work environment to keep you on track. You are a great idea person, but implementation gets away from you unless others help you ground the ideas. You have a great sensitivity for colors, sounds, scents, and so on, which may be a strength in your career. What you wear and how you arrange your home and work environment has a large impact on your well-being.

Friendships and romantic relationships are sacred to you, and you expect much from those you hold dear. You know how to listen deeply and carefully to others and how to give your undivided attention to make people feel seen and heard. More than other Pisces, you need to be cautious so that you don't lose yourself in other people's perspectives. Your mood governs your energy level, so keep in mind how much you'll be affected by other people's moods.

Libra rising with a Pisces Sun wants to express its magick through carving and dressing candles, creating sumptuous altars, writing beautiful invocations, or creating amazing ritual wear. You also know how to bring together people who use different types of magick and arrange smooth collaborations. You are good at spell work for making peace, laying spirits to rest, attracting familiars, and fostering self-love. Working with sound in magick and healing, whether it be voice, singing bowls, percussion, or an instrument, is also one of your gifts. You are especially good at performing rites of passage.

♏

Scorpio Rising

This rising increases your strength of character and the power to assert yourself. Although this is double water, your passions are so intense that you appear fiery. You live in the moment, but you want to know all the details and backstory that lead to each moment. When you are at your best, you are the brightest light or the darkest shadow in the room. If you feel blocked from reaching your goals, this combination can lead you to be seen as domineering or insensitive. Compromise does not come easily to you, but sarcasm does. Success in your work life depends on having backup plans for when you hit the wall. This is especially so because you are attracted to taking risks.

This much Scorpio and Pisces water creates an internal tension between being cruel or kind, open or secretive, affectionate, or aloof. Turn these tensions into shades of gray or, better yet, a full rainbow to access your power. You tend to have complicated friendships and relationships. Remind yourself that you chose many of the details that led to these beautiful and dramatic circumstances. You have a magnetic personality that draws people to you. You aren't alone, except when you choose to be.

Scorpio rising makes your energy capable of cutting through most energetic barriers. You can dissolve illusion or bring down wards or shields and see through to the truth. You may have an aptitude for breaking curses and lifting oppressive spiritual atmospheres. You have a knack for spells related to transformation, finding hidden or lost things, and revealing past lives. It is important that you do regular cleansing work for yourself. You are likely to end up doing messy work, and you do not have a nonstick aura. You would do well as a death midwife or a psychopomp. You may have a calling for working with dark forces and beings.

♐

Sagittarius Rising

This rising's enthusiasm and vision give you a boost in your outlook on life and confidence. The nonstop Sagittarius energy makes you more outgoing and playful than most Pisces. This combination doubles your generosity and desire to help people. Pisces follow their heart, but this rising adds interest in philosophy, ethics, and a broad understanding of the ways of the world. You love to travel and are equally interested in cultures, landscapes, and meeting new people. When you need to recharge fast, go outdoors; being outside lets you feel the interconnectedness of all living things.

Sagittarius wants freedom and adventure in relationships and prefers comfort and closeness. Whether it is friends or lovers, find the right proportion of these two ways of being. Both signs have a strong desire for connection but have very different approaches, so you must find a way to honor both. This combination makes you feel that the odds will be in your favor, and that inner guidance will lead the way. This is often true, and when it isn't, you'll pick yourself up and make it true. One of your saving graces is that you can find meaning and inspiration in almost anything.

Your magick is stronger when you are near fire or water. This could be a candle or a bowl of water, but a bonfire or a body of water is even better. Your rising sign's fire can become any shape or size you need. Skill in the use and creation of ritual tools is favored by this combination because you can push your energy and intentions into objects with ease. You have a talent for rituals and spells that call forth inspiration, break down obstacles, and offer thanks and gratitude. If you do astral travel or soul journeying, be sure all of you is back and in its proper place within you. You also are good at seeing through deceptive or stealth magick.

♑

Capricorn Rising

Serious, obsessive, and intense is just a normal day for you. You embrace struggles and challenges and laugh at obstacles because you get a great amount of satisfaction in proving your strength and merit. You like to be thought of as dependable, levelheaded, and a hard worker. You are among the most grounded of Pisces unless you allow pessimism to undermine you. Normally you give off an air of being calm and quietly in charge of your life. You'll know you've drifted too far into negative thinking when you start being harsh to the people around you. Peaceful and restful times are essential to your well-being; work can wait.

When you take a positive interest in specific people, it can be mutually beneficial. You tend to be a stabilizing influence in the lives of those you interact with. You are a good role model for perseverance and outcome setting. In matters of love or friendship, do not let worry over loss prevent you from sharing yourself with others. You are not as good a judge of character as you believe. Don't rely on first impressions or what people say about themselves. Observe their actions and the outcomes generated by their choices. Also, those close to you do not judge you as severely as you do yourself. You are a bit of a manipulator, but your motivations come from a place of wanting to be of service.

Capricorn rising creates an aura and energy field that is slow to come up to speed but has amazing momentum and force once fully activated. Try working with crystals, stones, even geographic features like mountains as your magick blends well with them. Your rituals and spells benefit from having a structure and a plan of action. Multipart spells done over time are often your best work. You are especially good at warding and spells to make long-term changes. Spells for prosperity and attracting business work well for you.

≈

Aquarius Rising

You are definitely quirkier and more unconventional than other Pisceans; you'll always make a splash. You have lots of areas of special interest, so the terms *geek* or *nerd* are probably appropriate and proudly claimed. Although you are forward thinking, your desire for certainty and purity in your beliefs and ideologies can get in the way of progress. Although you dislike being restricted or directed, you often have the urge to enforce your ideas on others. Aquarius likes to live in their thoughts and Pisces in their imagination, so it is easy to lose your anchoring to the world. Don't wander too long in these bright visions; bring them back to Earth to manifest them.

This combination makes for original thinking and moments of virtuosity that make you an excellent problem-solver. You may have a gift for technology or information management. Your expressive and creative speech make it easy to connect with people. It is harder for you to go from casual friendship to something deeper because you need to drop your act. This is hard because you are always on the alert, a bit hypervigilant, and you rebel against commitment. You enjoy traveling as much as you do kicking back at home. Friends and partners you can do both with are keepers.

Aquarius rising helps you consciously change the shape and density of your aura. This makes you a generalist who can adapt to many styles and forms of magick. Witchcraft focused on increasing intuition, analysis of problems, and release from emotional restrictions is supported by this combination. Visualization can play an important role in your magick and meditations. If you aren't particularly good at visualization, focus on the spoken word to tune in to your power. Aquarius rising is gifted at separating the useful from the outmoded in magick. You have a gift for spells that have tangible real-world results quickly.

♓
Pisces Rising

Your Pisces-inspired psychic perceptions connect you with all the life, energy, and spirits around you. You are guided and often protected, but don't make your spirit helpers work too hard. People are never quite sure what to expect as there is an almost mystical haze around you. Your changing moods can be a challenge to your loved ones; recognize that and be kind. You are kind and sweet and seem harmless enough, but you do hide a secret. You are slippery and mutable and want to be free to change your shape and flow wherever your wishes take you. If you are denied access to your mutable desires, everyone will be unhappy in the end.

Spirituality, magick, and religion have a profound impact on you and are involved in many of the turning points in your life. Faith in yourself or something greater is the source of your capacity to endure and persevere. When you run low on ambition or drive, look to your spirituality for your next goal. Also look to your loved ones and ask what they need. This is your route to being more practical. Music, and the arts in general, is the best medicine for your body, mind, and spirit.

Pisces rising amplifies your Pisces Sun's connection to the other planes of reality. Your power flows when you do magick to open the gates to the other worlds. You have a special gift for creating sacred space and blessing places. You can do astral travel, hedge riding, and soul travel in all their forms with some training and practice. You can help others find and develop their psychic gifts. Mental training to sharpen your powers of concentration is essential for you to reach your potential. Meditation, memory exercises, and visualization practices serve you well.

A DISH FIT FOR A PISCES:
LUSCIOUS LAYERS LOVING LASAGNA

Dawn Aurora Hunt

* * *

Are you ready to lose yourself in a mile-high lasagna? Nothing boring for you, my Piscean friend! For you, connection and caring for others is important, and with this dish, you will be able to bring everyone together as well as feed your own heart and soul. This classic dish melts in your mouth with a mystical mouthfeel from whipping the ricotta, while creamy layers of melty mozzarella bring joyful energy and emotional connections. Tomatoes hold the power of love to give and receive it in all forms. With each layer you build of this dish, visualize and meditate on learning to love yourself and to let others love you too. So, soak up that sauce and allow yourself to receive the love you so readily give to others.

Note: This dish can be made gluten-free by simply using gluten-free lasagna noodles in place of regular ones.

Ingredients:

- 2 tablespoons extra virgin olive oil
- 1 whole yellow onion, chopped
- 6 cloves garlic, minced
- 2 15-ounce cans whole plum tomatoes
- 1 8-ounce can tomato sauce
- Salt and pepper to taste
- ¼ cup fresh basil, chopped
- ¼ cup fresh Italian parsley, chopped
- 32-ounce whole milk ricotta cheese
- 8 ounces mascarpone cheese
- 8 ounces frozen spinach, thawed and drained
- 1 teaspoon granulated garlic
- 32-ounce no-boil lasagna noodles
- 16-ounce shredded mozzarella cheese
- 8-ounce fresh mozzarella cheese, sliced

Directions:

In a large saucepan, heat olive oil on medium heat. Add onions and garlic and sauté until fragrant and translucent. Add tomatoes and liquid into the pot. Using your hands, break up the tomatoes until they are slightly chunky. Add tomato sauce, salt, pepper, basil, and parsley and let simmer for about twenty to thirty minutes.

While the sauce is simmering, make the ricotta filling. Using a blender set on medium-low speed, whip together ricotta, mascarpone, spinach, granulated garlic, and salt and pepper to taste. Set aside.

When your sauce has reduced slightly, break up any remaining large pieces of tomato using a fork. Heat the oven to 375 degrees Fahrenheit. In a large, deep, oven-safe baking dish, begin to build your lasagna layers. Spray the bottom of the pan with cooking spray to prevent sticking. Then coat the bottom of the pan in a thin layer of sauce. In an even layer, place the no-boil lasagna noodles. Spoon more sauce over the noodles in a thin layer, then create a layer of ricotta cheese mixture using a teaspoon to dollop the mixture in even amounts spaced about two inches apart. Sprinkle shredded mozzarella on top of the ricotta layer. Add another layer of noodles and sauce and repeat this layering process until the pan is full or you have run out of ingredients. When you reach the top layer of noodles, lightly coat it in sauce. Evenly layer the sliced fresh mozzarella cheese and sprinkle with any remaining shredded cheese. Dust with granulated garlic, dried basil, and oregano if desired.

Cover with foil and bake for forty-five to sixty minutes, until slightly bubbling around the edges and all the cheese on the top/middle is melted. Remove from the oven and let rest ten to fifteen minutes before slicing and serving.

RECHARGING AND SELF-CARE

Mat Auryn

When it comes to recharging and self-care, we must allow ourselves to delve into our traits and tend to the areas where we might need a bit more help. By taking this balanced approach, you're sure to be able to relax and rejuvenate so that you can take on the world and aren't just surviving but thriving! As Pisces, it's easy to want to do the self-care that makes us feel good, like an escape. However, genuinely caring for ourselves also means giving time and focus to areas we might be resistant to but need to address so that we can function in society and create the security we so deeply need. Through this approach, we honor our mystical, dreamy, and escapist aspects by giving them time and attention so that they don't bleed over into other areas of our lives in a detrimental way. Along with all the ideas in this section, it's incredibly healthy for a Pisces to devote regular time to meditating.

Cleaning and Décor—
Making Your "Aquarium" Yours

Pisces thrive in environments that spark our imaginations. We need our houses, rooms, and environments to be sanctuaries that feel comforting, creative, dreamy, and mystical. This is particularly true regarding the bedroom and the bathroom, as those are our two main areas of escape and recharging. As Pisces, we tend to have a cluttered nature without realizing it. We hoard things we like, and we can be so distracted with whatever project we're engaged in, whether that's a productive one or not, that before we know it, a huge mess has quickly accumulated. Since we're so energetically sensitive, the environment of a room affects us in ways that are perhaps more intense than other signs. Not only is cleaning an essential task that we need to do to take care of ourselves, but decorating and creating a mood are equally important.

The bedroom should feel like a dreamy and mystical place of retreat. The bathroom should feel like our own private spa. Our office should inspire our creativity without creating a space of distraction (which can quickly happen with us).

Cleaning with Spirit

Cleaning and decorating can be a spiritual practice, which should already make it more appealing. Not only is it self-care, but it's a chance to do emotional reflection and to connect and honor the spirit of place. Before you begin, take a moment to go inward and connect to the spirit of your home and the spirit of that individual room. Tell it that your cleaning and decorating is an act of devotion toward it. When you get acquainted with the spirit of place and are in a good relationship with it, you will see that it will naturally bring comfort, happiness, and peace to you while in your home. You'll also find that your home will work on its own to protect you from outside energetic disturbances that might try to make their way in, including unwelcomed spirits.

As you clean and decorate, turn it into a moving meditation and spell. Think in terms of metaphor. What might the mess be symbolic of? After reflecting on it, think about what sort of intention cleaning it does. For example, if I have piles of dirty clothes on the floor, that might represent emotions I'm not comfortable wearing that I allow to pile up. By putting them in their clothing hamper and washing them, I symbolically intend to release and renew my emotional state. Likewise, dirty windows might symbolize how I view the outside world and how others view me. By cleaning them, I'm symbolically bringing clarity to my perception of the world and its perception of me. How you relate to the cleaning process is highly personal, with no wrong answers; the key is to think symbolically and act with intention.

Rub-a-Dub-Dub

While I'm sure they are out there, I have never met a Pisces who wasn't obsessed with taking baths to relax and recharge if they have access to a bathtub. When I take baths, I don't do so to get clean. I take showers for that. Baths are always spiritual for me, whether I'm taking a ritual bath or just treating the bath as a ritual of recharging self-care. So when it comes to your self-care baths, grab your scented candles, your bottle of bath bubbles, your Epsom salt soak, play some relaxing music, pour yourself a glass of wine, take that edible, and treat this as a time to honor yourself and indulge. This is the time to let out your merfolk form no one sees and escape the stress and burdens of the human world.

Catharsis

As water signs, we already know that we're incredibly emotional. Being able to express our emotions in healthy and appropriate ways helps us gain more control over them so that they aren't overwhelming us, we aren't bottling them up or, at worst, letting them control us. If you can afford therapy or counseling, I highly recommend it. There's a stigma around both, but we need to break that. Therapy and counseling help us create emotional and psychological health and give us a safe space to explore our emotions. These are things that I feel are important for any witch, but even more so for the Pisces witch. However, not all of us can afford those. There are still many ways we can explore and express our emotions healthily. Having a close friend you trust and explore your emotions with can be incredibly healing. Most of all, journaling is crucial for us. Having a journal allows us to explore our emotions and express them in absolute privacy.

Writing out what you're feeling is cathartic, allowing us to take those inner emotions and externalize them. I know that for myself, I often feel things before I can articulate or express them, especially the why. If I'm upset and someone asks me what's wrong, I sometimes don't know what to say as I feel things first, and I feel things intensely. The act of journaling allows you to articulate those feelings and explore why you might be feeling them.

Life Is Like a Dream, and Dream Is Like a Life

Sleep is my favorite form of self-care as a Pisces. Sleeping and dreaming are the ultimate escapism that are not only healthy but crucial for human health in almost all areas. Specifically, for dreamy fish, it's healthy for us to have a very active dream life while we're asleep, especially since we're often very talented at lucid dreaming. Being unable to dream often or having difficulty remembering our dreams can cause two blockages. First, dreaming is a way to process our day-to-day life, including its stresses and other emotions. Second, some of our most potent guidance, spiritual insight, and psychic messages can occur in our dreams. So we want to ensure that when our heads hit that pillow, we engage in a very active dream life. Aside from diet and exercise, one of the most common reasons one can have difficulty dreaming is lack of sleep. The body prioritizes resting, healing, and rejuvenating the body, then proceeds to process our mental and emotional life through dreams. Therefore, ensuring that you're getting good sleep and a healthy amount of it is essential to induce dreams. I'm also a huge fan of power naps throughout the day and will wake up feeling like I've fully recharged.

Relaxing to Dream

When you lie down to go to bed at night, simply bring your awareness to your body. Focus on one part of your body at a time. Start with your feet, moving up to your head and face. While you focus on that part of your body, command it to relax and release tension. When your physical body is relaxed, you'll fall asleep much quicker.

Floating Your Day Away

After you've fully relaxed, mentally review your day, starting from when you woke up to now. As you review each part, particularly the parts that frustrate, stress, or evoke strong emotions from you, simply deeply exhale. As you do so, imagine your breath is filling a balloon and, along with it, the situation. The balloon immediately ties shut after your exhale and floats away to outer space. Once you've reached the part of your day where you're lying down to go to sleep, if you've made it this far without falling asleep, you should be emotionally and mentally relaxed enough to be able to dream with a more substantial chance that the dreams won't be processing your day.

Water, Water Everywhere, and Not a Drop to Drink

Most people don't get nearly enough water in their day. By consciously choosing to stay hydrated and monitoring our sodium intake, we also increase our vital energy throughout the day, which fights fatigue and brain fog. Staying well hydrated is vital for everyone of any sign. However, I highly recommend staying extra hydrated for psychic and magickal purposes, which makes it extra important for a Pisces. Water is energetically receptive. So by staying well hydrated, we increase our receptivity to energy and psychic and intuitive information. Not only that, but water keeps our energy systems flowing.

No Place Like Home Frequency

My husband, Devin Hunter, teaches a technique called Finding Your Home Frequency.[6] It's a powerful concept that has

---

6. Devin Hunter, *The Witch's Book of Power* (Woodbury, MN: Llewellyn Publications, 2016).

transformed my life and spirituality as a Pisces. Each person's home frequency is unique and represents the frequency of their personal energy. For Pisces witches, who often absorb others' energies, this practice serves as a reminder of our personal "home base" frequency, like a default setting for our spirit. In his writing, Devin explains that the home frequency is the most perfect state of oneself— a psychic, mental, and physical state of balance and abundance. Entering the home frequency means reenchanting oneself and returning to our own energetic signature, free from external influences.

Understanding our personal home frequency allows us to navigate and align with our environment. We can recognize when we or our surroundings are out of sync and compare the energies around us to our own ideal state. This awareness empowers us to override unstable environments and make conscious shifts in our own energy. To practice Finding Your Home Frequency, find a comfortable position and close your eyes. Take deep, relaxing breaths, visualizing the inhalations filling your body with divine energy and exhaling tensions and negativity. Allow thoughts to come and go like passing clouds, returning your focus to the exercise. Next, conjure memories of confident, happy, loving moments, and re-create those emotions within yourself. Feel the positive energy flow through you, releasing any bonds holding you back. Focus on the divinity and perfection of your soul, visualizing it as a light within and around you. With intention, spread this light into your surroundings. When you're done, return your thoughts to your body and open your eyes, feeling the difference within yourself and your environment.

Mastering this practice may require multiple attempts, but with time, you'll recognize your personal home frequency. Understanding your energy signature will enhance your psychic, intuitive, and empathic abilities, helping you discern what is truly you and what isn't. Eventually, you'll be able to shift to your home frequency at will just by thinking about it.

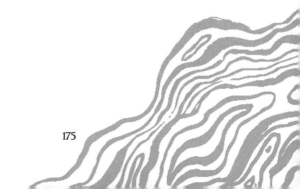

Tending the Tender

H. Byron Ballard

If you have tender feet or tend toward sore throats and earaches, you might be a Pisces. If you feel everyone else's pain but use alcohol, sex, or chocolate to avoid your own, you might be a Pisces. If you are a chameleon who can be whatever you are needed to be but often get lost in the day-to-day slog, you might be a Pisces. In these challenging times, we are sometimes best described as a mess, a hot mess.

Stop, dear one. Sit down in your favorite chair with a cup of tea and we will look at some ways to take care of ourselves in a world that loves to take bites out of our exquisite fins. Here's a plate of little sandwiches—some are jam, some are soft cheese, all are on rich brown bread. Jam for you? And a cheesy one too? Wonderful.

The keys to our Piscean self-care are threefold. We need to tend to our bodies, our emotions, and our souls.

We'll start with feet and work our way up and around the Piscean frame. We will always do best when attention is paid to our sensual nature. Don't get me wrong. That sort of delicious indulgence strokes our need for sensation, but when carried too far (another Piscean trait), it can lead us down a path of ill health. That sensuality can also lend itself to hedonism and self-indulgence and those, in turn, can drive us to punish ourselves for being "bad." An unhealthy cycle, to be sure.

Find ways to indulge your sybaritic nature by scheduling long swims and gentle hikes, luxuriating in soaking tubs of herb-scented water. Soak your feet in warm Epsom salts as often as you can, and always wrap your throat in soft wool when a chill wind is rising.

Boundaries are rarely part of the Pisces temperament, but cultivating safe space from which to interact with the world will allow more freedom to love spontaneously without setting your generous heart up for another hard fall. Learn your emotional triggers and give yourself permission to step behind a flowering and thorny hedge to think about your personal history. Take deep breaths and ground your watery self into the soil beneath your feet. Then remind yourself that the needy, sexy dumpster fire luring you to the rescue is not your twin flame.

Pisces's link to the spiritual encompasses mainstream religion as well as the more esoteric. We weave our spirit-filled world with divine beings, ancestors, land spirits, ghosts, and the lot. Our own souls seem only lightly tattooed on our bodies, able to stretch away from the physical in search of the numinous. Allow yourself the pleasure of a regular spiritual practice that centers and nourishes your bright pilgrim soul.

Let's braid these three threads together into a plaited Piscean self-blessing. When you stand under the flow of the shower or slip your shoulders under the water of your bath, speak some words of bliss over your body, your heart, and your soul. Find the words that speak comfort and inspiration so that you emerge from the water with the strength and courage we all need to go forth.

The water cleanses me, body, soul, and spirit.
The water blesses me, without and within.
The water sustains me, resilient and everlasting.
Where the water is, there am I.
Where I am, water is also there.
Heart and soul and blessed body, water upholds you,
*   nurtures you, and heals you. Heals me.*
Blessed be the waters, and blessed be all we.

DON'T BLAME IT
ON YOUR SUN SIGN

Mat Auryn

I t's so easy to fall into the trap of blaming things on being a Pisces that reinforces its stereotypes and detrimental qualities—and Pisces is in no short supply of them. These qualities can include escapism, indecisiveness, laziness, naivety, being overly sensitive and scatterbrained, a lack of boundaries, self-pity, and martyrdom. These issues are rooted in emotions, particularly the gratification and prioritization of emotions over everything else. While these are issues we are predisposed to as Pisces, we can't use our Sun sign to excuse such traits and behaviors. Instead, we should reframe them as the challenges we need to address.

Almost all of Pisces's main negative qualities can be boiled down to a concept coined by psychoanalyst Carl Jung as *puer aeternus* and *puella aeterna*, which means the "eternal boy" and "eternal girl," respectively. This idea is sometimes commonly known as Peter Pan Syndrome in pop psychology. As Pisces, we tend to want to escape the real world and the adult responsibilities of it. Peter Pan Syndrome is defined as a desire not to want to grow up, just as Peter Pan actively fights against adulthood as the enemy and desires to escape the real world and live eternally in Neverland, the land of the imagination and delight. However, we can quickly find that Neverland becomes more akin to Pleasure Island of Pinocchio, where the desire to escape into one's childlike indulgences becomes a trap that turns us into jackasses.

This escapism can present itself in numerous ways for Pisces. This can be through addiction, obsession, lack of self-control, and neglect to prioritize responsibility. Pair this with emotional elements, and these vices seem almost entirely overwhelming. *Addiction* is one of the first keywords you will find when looking up the negative qualities of a Pisces, and I've found it to be true. This can be an addiction to substances that allow one to escape and promote feelings of well-being. Almost all addiction has an emotional component to it, and often addicts struggle against emotional trauma that they don't feel equipped to handle. This is particularly difficult for the Pisces because they want to immerse themselves deeply into everything, making placing a boundary on excess seemingly impossible. This addictive quality isn't just lim-ited to substance abuse. We can find it in obsessive behavior that serves as escapism, whether that's expressed as an addiction to social media, video games, television, unhealthy romantic obsessions, emotional eating, or anything where we can immerse ourselves so deeply that we struggle to take control and responsibility for ourselves and our actions for a quick fix of dopamine.

Navigating the Never-Ending Labyrinth of Life

A fantastic portrayal of the challenges of a Pisces is the character of Sarah (played by Jennifer Connelly) in Jim Henson and Brian Froud's fantasy cult classic *Labyrinth*. The movie's theme revolves around growing up when you don't want to. In the process, Sarah realizes that specific aspects and qualities of childhood repurposed adequately are crucial for navigating life. This provides the key to Pisces's remedy to the above issues.

The movie begins with Sarah immersing herself in roleplay in a manner considered by most of society a bit too childish for her age. Noteworthy is that she's roleplaying an adult, mirroring the images of her mother on her makeup mirror.

She then is forced (to her protesting) to put her baby brother (symbolic of her inner child) to bed—which is when the adventure starts. Her little brother, Toby, is throwing a tantrum like babies do, exactly when Sarah is also throwing a childish tantrum for having to take care of the baby. Once she puts the baby to bed is when the quest to find her inner child starts. The whole quest is a battle against the clock that the goblin king Jareth (played by David Bowie) presents before she enters the Labyrinth, a fight against the inevitability of time itself when childhood must end.

Throughout the movie, she's confronted with aspects of her childhood. The items and toys we see in her room at the beginning appear as characters and settings within the Labyrinth itself. She quickly finds that the adult approach of thinking logically and trying to rationalize everything rarely solves any of the demanding situations when she thinks it can—in fact, it often makes the situation worse or more confusing. She only solves each challenge through creative, intuitive, and playful approaches while learning the importance of responsibility and facing things she doesn't want to. Sarah learns that she doesn't have to face life alone, but that she ultimately must face it—and that doing so doesn't mean that she must lose her inner child, but instead find her appreciation of it and its proper application within her life. The whole movie seemingly takes place in Sarah's imagination. This is emphasized by the fact that she's reading a book called *Labyrinth* while roleplaying at the beginning of the movie, where she recites the final lines of power that she speaks in the movie to Jareth.

Another fantastic example of this is another fantasy cult classic, the novel (and movie) *The Neverending Story*, where the main character, Bastian, is escaping his bullies, the depression of his home life, and the responsibilities of school to immerse himself in a novel. As he gets lost in the book, he realizes there's a link between himself and the story. He confronts the issues of his own life through this escapism, and as the main character, Atreyu, grows and learns lessons, he also grows and learns. While the movie cuts the novel off short, at the end of the novel, Bastian has grown so much through the experiences of Atreyu (and then later himself when he literally enters the story itself) that he has learned how to face life instead of escaping it.

Turn Your Escapist Imagination into a Hypersigil of Transformation

Just as Sarah and Bastian used their immersive imagination to face the responsibilities and boundaries they were escaping in real life, we can also do that. This is a great way to take the qualities holding us back in life and repurpose them into strengths—and this is the heart of shadow work. One effective method we can utilize is through a magickal practice known as hypersigils. The term *hypersigil* was introduced by Grant Morrison, a graphic novelist and chaos magician. He stumbled upon this idea while conducting an experiment with his comic book series *The Invisibles*. Morrison noticed that any actions he performed on a character based on himself in the series manifested in his own life.

A hypersigil builds upon the concept of a sigil. A sigil is a symbol representing energetic power and intended to bring about magickal transformations in the magician's life. However, a hypersigil goes beyond a mere two-dimensional glyph by incorporating characters and a storyline. Essentially, it involves utilizing imagination, creativity, and emotions as tools for instigating change. This approach is particularly suitable for Pisces folk, as it aligns with our inclination to escape into fantasy and fully immerse ourselves in its creation, sometimes to the point of obsession. It's important that the story evoke strong emotions. If the term *hypersigil* is confusing, just ignore it. In essence, it's an act of sympathetic magick using storytelling as the spell.

While writing your story, let your imagination take over. Create a character who represents you, describing them as you would yourself. Create characters and challenges representing the qualities you want to overcome and change in your life and find creative ways to overcome them. For example, in *The Neverending Story*, depression and nihilism are represented as the Swamps of Sadness that Atreyu must travel through. In *Labyrinth*, the Junk Lady tries to trap Sarah in a re-creation of her room full of her childhood materialism. In both cases, the character overcomes it and comes out stronger because of it. It's crucial to be aware that while writing your fantasy story, you are engaging in a magickal act of self-transformation. Just like a poppet, what you do to your character will happen to you, so also be cautious and mindful of what occurs to your character.

Adulting Made Easier for Pisces

Another great approach for taking responsibilities for our negative qualities is to reframe how we're approaching it. Just as Sarah discovered that she needed to protect and rescue her inner child, we can also take this approach instead of neglecting and abandoning it altogether. We can protect that inner child that is so crucial for a Pisces's powers and strengths by approaching life as being our own parent. Proper parenting ensures that a child's most essential needs are met and taken care of through responsibility. A great guardian also teaches a child how to own up to their flaws and mistakes in a healthy manner that assists them in character development. Most of all, a parent will tell a child no when they just want to play instead of performing a task like cleaning their room or when moderation needs to be enforced for the child's own good, such as eating a healthy meal when the child just wants to eat cake instead.

When you're forced to do "adulting" in ways you're resistant to, engage in a mental exercise where you pretend that you are your own ideal parent, where your embrace of responsibility isn't about abandoning your childlike nature, but rather a form of protecting and taking care of it so that you have the freedom and comfort in your life to engage in that side of yourself when it's proper and healthy to do so. Also, learn to take emotional responsibility for yourself by tapping into your deep empathy. Consider how what you do makes others feel by pretending someone else is doing it to you. How would you want the other person to rectify, own up to, and change? Be completely honest about this, and you'll find rapid personal growth.

Make this process of adulting an act of meditative role-play. This can also be deeply healing, as your primary motive for engaging in this exercise is your deep love and desire to take care of your inner child, perhaps in ways many of us didn't have while growing up.

POSTCARD FROM A PISCES WITCH

Heron Michelle

She must be an old soul, they'd say, a daydreamer, a precocious, an oddly independent child. I was born March 7, 1974, under the twilight balance of a Pisces sunset and her rising Virgo full Moon. This granted me a vivid imagination, creative curiosity, and an easy empathy with the world around me. Though my Piscean perceptions weren't always shared within the conservative Christian home of my childhood in Taylors, South Carolina.

As far back as I can remember, I could "see" and feel the energy connections between everything. I saw "halos" of colorful energy flowing through everything and would play with moving the colors with my mind. I had the typical psychic intuition, dreaming prolifically, sometimes about future happenings. Other dreams were through the eyes of different people in past times and places I had no logical way of knowing; those felt more like memories. As young as three years old, I was consciously aware that just around that last bend in the road, I'd been an adult male around thirty years old with a wife I'd loved passionately. I'd been an American soldier during World War I, dying in France. I remember the adrenaline of warfare, the feel of the rifle and bayonet in my hands, and an explosion causing rubble to trap me under a slow, suffocating death. I still occasionally panic from claustrophobia.

Despite all my years spent in Church pews, I steadfastly understood reincarnation as the truest thing. I'd chosen to return to this middle world, and this specific family, with a purpose to fulfill. That much I knew for certain. This knowing gave me a stubborn insistence that I should have full sovereignty over my life choices. With 100 percent surety, I knew that the divine spirit I remembered from between lifetimes was pure bliss, unconditional love, and complete acceptance. So, I automatically dismissed all notions of sexism, racism, or homophobia as ludicrous sacrilege.

Training in witchcraft eventually honed my Piscean clairvoyance so I could slip into a waking trance at will. I learned to astral travel beyond the liminal veil of illusion, to seek spiritual partnerships and "distance view" anywhere in time and imagination. The besom I've learned to fly is more like a time machine! However, it was the tools of Reiki energy healing that enabled me to connect to specific people, places, and objects; through interconnection, I could experience their history, emotions, and purpose. Reiki taught me to focus divine energy at the source of wounds, anywhere through time and space. Taken a step further, this practice enabled me to retrieve detailed past-life information and to ease the traumatic impact of those past lives in the present. Through my Pisces witching work, I've affirmed for myself that the occult reality is our oneness within the god/dess of nature. Their magick of divine love is our inheritance if we can only imagine such wondrous gifts. Having a Piscean imagination certainly helps!

SPIRIT OF PISCES GUIDANCE RITUAL

Ivo Dominguez, Jr.

The signs are more than useful constructs in astrology or categories for describing temperaments, they are also powerful and complicated spiritual entities. So, what is meant when we say that a sign is a spirit? I often describe the signs of the zodiac as the twelve forms of human wisdom and folly. The signs are twelve styles of human consciousness, which also means that the signs are well-developed group minds and egregores. Think on the myriad of people over thousands of years who have poured energy into the constructs of the signs through intentional visualization and study. Moreover, the lived experience of each person as one of the signs is deposited into the group minds and egregores of their sign. Every Pisces who has ever lived or is living contributes to the spirit of Pisces.

The signs have a composite nature that allows them to exist in many forms on multiple planes of reality at once. In addition to the human contribution to their existence, the spirits of the signs are made from inputs from all living beings in our world whether they are made of dense matter or spiritual substances. These vast and ancient thought-forms that became group minds and then egregores are also vessels that can be used by divine beings to communicate with humans as well. The spirits of the signs can manifest themselves as small as a sprite or larger than the Earth. The shape and the magnitude of the spirit of Pisces emerging before you will depend on who you are and how and why you call upon them.

Purpose and Use

This ritual will make it possible to commune with the spirit of Pisces. The form that the spirit will take will be different each time you perform the ritual. What appears will be determined by what you are looking for and your state of mind and soul. The process for preparing yourself for the ritual will do you good as well. Aligning yourself with the source and core of your energy is a useful practice in and of itself. Exploring your circumstances, motivations, and intentions is a valuable experience whether or not you are performing this ritual.

If you have a practical problem that you are trying to solve or an obstacle that must be overcome, the spirit of Pisces may have useful advice. If you are trying to better understand who you are and what you are striving to accomplish, then the spirit of Pisces can be your mentor. Should you have a need to recharge yourself or flush out stale energy, you can use this ritual to reconnect with a strong clear current of power that is compatible with your core. This energy can be used for magickal empowerment, physical vitality, and healing or redirected for spell work. If you are charging objects or magickal implements with Pisces energy, this ritual can be used for this purpose as well.

Timing for the Ritual

The prevailing astrological conditions have an impact on how you experience a ritual, the type and amount of power available, and the outcomes of the work. If you decide you want to go deeper in your studies of astrology, you'll find many techniques to pick the best day and time for your ritual. Thankfully, the ritual to meet the spirit of your sign does not require exact timing or perfect astrological conditions. This ritual depends on your inner connection to your Sun sign, so it is not as reliant on the external celestial conditions as some other rituals. Each of us has worlds within ourselves, which include inner landscapes and inner skies. Your birth chart, and the sky that it depicts, shines brightest within you. Although not required, you can improve the effectiveness of this ritual if you use any of the following simple guidelines for favorable times:

- When the Moon or the Sun is in Pisces.
- When Jupiter is in Pisces.
- On Thursday, the day of Jupiter, and even better at dawn, which is its planetary hour.
- When the Sun is in or near 15 degrees of Pisces.
- When the Moon is conjunct Neptune in any sign.

Materials and Setup

The following is a description of the physical objects that will make it easier to perform this ritual. Don't worry if you don't have all of them, as in a pinch, you need no props. However, the physical objects will help to anchor the energy and your mental focus.

You will need:

- ✦ A printout of your birth chart
- ✦ A table to serve as an altar
- ✦ A chair if you want to sit during the ritual
- ✦ A small bowl of water with the addition of a tiny pinch of sea salt and/or a small seashell
- ✦ An assortment of items for the altar that correspond to Pisces or Neptune or Jupiter (an amethyst or lepidolite, a seashell with a spiral such as a conch or whelk, gardenias, or willow leaves and twigs)
- ✦ A pad and a pen or chalk and a small blackboard

Instructions:

Before beginning the ritual, you may wish to copy the ritual invocations onto paper or bookmark this chapter and bring the book into the ritual. I find that the process of writing out the invocation, whether hand-written or typed, helps forge a better connection with the words and their meaning. If possible, put the altar table in the center of your space, and if not, then as close to due east as you can manage. Place the bowl with the water on the altar and hold your hand over it. Send warming energy from your hand to the water. Put your birth chart on the altar to one side of the bowl and arrange the items that you have selected to anchor the Pisces and planetary energy around it. To the other side of the bowl, place the pad and pen. Make sure you turn off your phone, close the door, close the curtains, or do whatever else is needed to prevent distractions.

Ritual to Meet the Spirit of Your Sign

You may stand or be seated—whichever is the most comfortable for you. Begin by focusing on your breathing. When you pay attention to the process of breathing, you become more aware of your body, the flow of your life energy, and the balance between conscious and unconscious actions. After you have done so for about a minute, it is time to shift into fourfold breathing. This consists of four phases: inhaling, lungs full, exhaling, and lungs empty. You count to keep time so that each of the four phases is of equal duration. Try a count of four or five in your first efforts. Depending on your lungs and how fast you count, you will need to adjust the number higher or lower. When you hold your breath, hold it with your belly muscles, not your throat. When you hold your breath in fourfold breathing, your throat should feel relaxed. Be gentle and careful with yourself if you have asthma, high blood pressure, are late in pregnancy, or have any other condition that may have an impact upon your breathing and blood pressure. In general, if there are difficulties, they arise during the lungs full or empty phases because of holding them by clenching the throat or compressing the lungs. The empty and the full lungs should be held by the position of the diaphragm, and the air passages left open. After one to three minutes of fourfold breathing, you can return to your normal breathing pattern.

Now close your eyes and move your center of consciousness down into the middle of your chest. Proceed with grounding and centering, dropping and opening, shifting into the alpha state, or whatever practice you use to reach the state of mind that supports ritual work. Then gaze deeply inside yourself and find yourself sitting on the ground in a garden under a velvety star-filled sky. Take a breath and smell fresh air and sweet fragrances on the evening breeze. Let the beauty of the night awaken all the places and spaces within you that are of Pisces. When you feel ready, open your eyes.

Zodiac Casting

If you are seated, stand if you are able and face the east. Slowly read this invocation aloud, putting some energy into your words. As you read it, slowly turn counterclockwise so that you come full circle when you reach the last line. Another option is to hold your hand over your head and trace the counterclockwise circle of the zodiac with your finger.

I call forth the twelve to join me in this rite.
I call forth Aries and the power of courage.
I call forth Taurus and the power of stability.
I call forth Gemini and the power of versatility.
I call forth Cancer and the power of protection.
I call forth Leo and the power of the will.
I call forth Virgo and the power of discernment.
I call forth Libra and the power of harmony.
I call forth Scorpio and the power of renewal.
I call forth Sagittarius and the power of vision.
I call forth Capricorn and the power of
    responsibility.
I call forth Aquarius and the power of
    innovation.
I call forth Pisces and the power of compassion.
The power of the twelve is here.
Blessed be!

Take a few deep breaths and gaze at the bowl of water. Become aware of the changes in the atmosphere around you and the presence of the twelve signs.

Altar Work
Pick up the printout of your birth chart and look at your chart. Touch each of the twelve houses with your

finger and push energy into them. You are energizing and awakening your birth chart to act as a focal point of power on the altar. Put your chart back on the altar when it feels ready to you. Then take the pad and pen and write the glyph for Pisces again and again. The glyphs can be different sizes, they can overlap, you can make any pattern with them you like so long as you pour energy into the ink as you write. Scribing the glyph is an action that helps draw the interest of the spirit of Pisces. Periodically look at the water in the bowl as you continue scribing the glyph. When you feel sensations in your body such as electric tingles, warmth, shivers, or something that you associate with the approach of a spirit, it is time to move on to the next step. If these are new experiences for you, just follow your instincts. Put away the pen and paper and pick up the sheet with the invocation of Pisces.

Invoking Pisces

Before beginning to read this invocation, get in touch with your feelings. Think on what you hope to accomplish in this ritual and why it matters to you. Then speak these lines slowly and with conviction.

Pisces, hear me, for I am born of the wide seas
　　of mutable water.
Pisces, see me, for the Pisces Sun shines
　　upon me.
Pisces, know me as a member of your family
　　and your company.
Pisces, know me as your student and your
　　protégé.
Pisces, know me as a conduit for your power.
Pisces, know me as a wielder of your magick.
I am of you, and you are of me.
I am of you, and you are of me.
I am of you, and you are of me.
Pisces is here within and without.
Blessed be!

Your Requests

Now look inward for several deep breaths and silently or aloud welcome the spirit of Pisces. Dip a finger into the bowl of water and draw it out. Close your eyes and ask for any guidance that would be beneficial for you and listen. It may take some time before anything comes through, so be patient. I find it valuable to receive guidance before making a request so that I can refine or modify intentions and outcomes. Consider the meaning of whatever impressions or guidance you received and reaffirm your intentions and desired outcomes for this ritual.

It is more effective to use multiple modes of communication to make your request. Speak silently or aloud the words that describe your need and how it could be solved. Visualize the same message but without the words and project the images on your mind's screen. Then put all your attention on your feelings and your bodily sensations that have been stirred up by contemplating your appeal to the spirit of Pisces. Once again wait and use all your physical and psychic senses to perceive what is given. At this point in the ritual if there are objects to be charged, touch them or focus your gaze on them.

Offer Gratitude

You may be certain or uncertain about the success of the ritual or the time frame for the outcomes to become clear. Regardless of that, it is a good practice to offer thanks and gratitude to the spirit of Pisces for being present. Also, thank yourself for doing your part of the work. The state of heart and mind that comes with thanks and gratitude makes it easier for the work to become manifest. Thanks and gratitude also act as a buffer against the unintended consequences that can be put into motion by rituals.

Release the Ritual

If you are seated, stand if you are able and face the east. Slowly turn clockwise until you come full circle while repeating the following or something similar.

> *Return, return oh turning wheel to your*
> *starry home.*
> *Farewell, farewell wise Pisces until we speak*
> *again.*

Another option while saying these words is to hold your hand over your head and trace a clockwise circle of the zodiac with your finger. When you are done, look at the altar and say,

> *It is done. It is done. It is done.*

Afterward

I encourage you to write down your thoughts and observations of what you experienced in the ritual. Do this while it is still fresh in mind before the details begin to blur. The information will become more useful over time as you work more with the spirit of Pisces. It will also let you evaluate the outcomes of your workings and improve your process in future workings. This journaling will also help you dial in any changes or refinements to this ritual for future use. Contingent upon the guidance you received or the outcomes you desire, you may want to add reminders to your calendar.

More Options

These are some modifications to this ritual that you may wish to try:

* Put together or purchase Pisces incense to burn during the ritual. A Pisces oil to anoint yourself or add to the water is another possibility. I'm providing one of my oil recipes as a possibility.
* Set up a richer and deeper altar. In addition to adding more objects that resonate

to the energy of Pisces, Neptune, or Jupiter, consecrate each object before the ritual. You may also want to place an altar cloth on the table that suggests Pisces, Neptune, or the element of water.

+ Creating a sigil to concentrate the essence of what you are working toward would be a good addition to the altar.

+ Consider adding chanting, free-form toning, or movement to raise energy for the altar work and/or for invoking Pisces.

+ If you feel inspired, you can write your own invocations for calling the zodiac and/or invoking Pisces. This is a great way to deepen your understanding of the signs and to personalize your ritual.

Rituals have greater personal meaning and effectiveness when you personalize them and make them your own.

PISCES ANOINTING OIL RECIPE

* * *

Ivo Dominguez, Jr.

This oil is used for charging and consecrating candles, crystals, and other objects you use in your practice. This oil makes it easier for an object to be imbued with Pisces energy. It also primes and tunes the objects so that your will and power as a Pisces witch flow more easily into it. Do not apply the oil to your skin unless you have done an allergy test first.

Ingredients:
- Carrier oil—1 ounce
- Myrrh—6 drops
- Vanilla—5 drops
- Vetiver—4 drops
- Jasmine—4 drops
- Sandalwood—3 drops

Instructions:

Pour one ounce of a carrier oil into a small bottle or vial. The preferred carrier oils are almond oil or fractionated coconut oil. Other carrier oils can be used. If you use olive oil, the blend will have a shorter shelf life. Ideally use essential oils, but fragrance oils can be used as substitutes. Add the drops of the essential oils into the carrier. Once they are all added, cap the bottle tightly, and shake the bottle several times. Hold the bottle in your hands, take a breath, and pour energy into the oil. Visualize blue-green energy or repeat the word *Pisces* or raise energy in your preferred manner. Continue doing so until it feels warm, seems to glow, or you sense that it is charged.

Label the bottle and store the oil in a cool, dark, place. Consider keeping a little bit of each previous batch of oil to add to the new batch. This helps build the strength and continuity of the energy and intentions you have placed in the oil. Over time that link makes your oils more powerful.

• BETTER EVERY DAY: THE WAY FORWARD •

Mat Auryn

As magickal practitioners, we can underestimate the role that being a Pisces plays in our magick and energy work. Just as the Sun is the primary source of light and power in our solar system, the Sun in our chart signifies how our purpose and power are manifested within our personality and life and how our magick organically operates. Psychologist Carl Jung utilized astrology to get an idea of his patients' personalities. He would find consistent correlations between what his clients were going through and their astrological charts, to the point of saying they were meaningful coincidences, or rather synchronicities. He believed that one's astrological chart provided information about a person's personality and psyche and was essentially a blueprint of the soul's plan for incarnation.

Pisces isn't just an identity; it's also a vision of the possibilities our souls can accomplish in this lifetime. Knowing your Piscean nature can be advantageous in terms of magick, as it allows you to identify your magickal strengths and weaknesses and work to overcome or cultivate them accordingly. We have a particular set of gifts, sensitivities, and challenges that we must face. These skill sets and sensitivities can be used to tap into an ocean's depth of magickal and mystical potential, or they can cause us to drown and lose ourselves if we aren't mindful. As a Pisces, you can tap into your unique psychic and intuitive gifts to help others. With the proper guidance and practice, you can find your authentic voice and use it to impact your own life and the life of others positively.

Witchcraft is about developing an understanding of ourselves and the people, forces, and nature surrounding us. Connecting with both the spirit of Pisces and the archetypal characteristics of Pisces, absorbing their lessons, and consciously applying their energy is sure to lead to a deeper connection with ourselves and our magickal abilities.

Emotional Intuitive Witchery

One of the most vital components for a Pisces witch regarding spellcasting is the emotional component. Like all water signs, we feel emotions intensely. This intensity is a power source that will strengthen your magick. A Pisces's magick should move them so strongly that it encourages the universe itself to move along with those currents of energy. This means that the emotional body should be going through profound shifts while casting and adapting one's spells to reflect this intuitively.

That intuition will inform you whether your words should be a whisper or a roar. It will turn simple spoken words into ones coated in honey or drenched in vinegar as they leave your mouth to paint the air. Your intuition will inform you to do certain gestures and movements while engaged in ritual. It will turn old dusty printed words into something alive and powerful. However, these things must be genuinely felt for the Pisces, which includes tuning in to your own emotional body, conjuring up that emotional feeling, and imbuing it in your magickal acts. Pair this emotional energy with pure willpower and a powerful imagination, and others will be amazed at what the simplest spells can do for you.

Don't Lose Yourself—Cautionary Tales

Like many other children of my generation, we had *The Rainbow Fish* by Marcus Pfister read to us in kindergarten. The story is about a fish with beautiful rainbow scales. The other fish envy Rainbow Fish, and all shun him unless he gives them his scales. Eventually, an octopus advises Rainbow Fish to do just that, and Rainbow Fish gives away one of his scales to every fish until they're all the same. The message is supposed to be about the beauty of sharing, but Pisces should see this as a cautionary tale. Pisces is known to give away too much of themselves to others, to the point of martyrdom and self-depletion. Perhaps if the story was about giving away something other than pieces of himself, the message might be a bit better.

Unfortunately, Rainbow Fish is more concerned about how others feel about him than how he feels about himself. He gives away so much of himself that he's no longer the unique Rainbow Fish but now the same as everyone else. He has given in to peer pressure, and he has blindly accepted the "wisdom" of another in pure naivety instead of questioning it. I'm sure you can see how all of these are the obstacles of a Pisces.

Another similar story with a message that should serve as a warning to Pisces is the original version of *The Little Mermaid* by Hans Christian Andersen. Like the famous Disney version of the story, the little mermaid falls in love and, to win the affection of another, strikes a deal with a sea witch to give up her voice and her identity as a mermaid to become a human with feet. But, unlike the Disney version, it doesn't end happily ever after. Instead, the prince ends up marrying another woman, and the little mermaid dies, dissolving into sea-foam.

Luring Your Energy Back Spell

It's not uncommon for Pisces to give away too much of their energy or power to others, places, or events in your life. With this spell, you will be calling back your full power, grabbing it, and proclaiming your wholeness. This spell will help you reclaim your power and draw it back to you. Call back all aspects of yourself and your energy that you have given away, whether intentionally or unintentionally. Reclaim your wholeness and stand in your power with this spell.

You will need:
  ⋄ A white candle

Instructions:
Ground and center yourself. Take a moment to meditate on any moments where you may have given away too much of your energy or power to another. Visualize that energy in your mind turning into a small glowing fish that begins to encircle the candle, empowering it. Try to think of up to three times you've given away your power and leave it at that; you can always return to this working again. When you're done, visualize a small group of these fish, which represent parts of your

energy and power that you may have unconsciously given away, now returning. Sometimes, certain parts of our energy or power may never return, and we need to learn from that. So don't freak out if a fish refuses to return to your candle. Take a moment to realize how this event shaped who you are today, knowing that even without it, you are whole and complete just as you are and fully capable of moving forward in power.

When you are ready to light your candle, do so and say,

> *Candle glow and candle burn*
> *Scattered energy, now return*
> *I am whole and I am healed*
> *By my will, the spell is sealed.*

Just Keep Swimming!

Being highly emotional and sensitive, Pisces can run the risk of quickly falling into a downward spiral of self-destruction if they're not careful. As a witch, I am a firm believer in the power of positive thinking and that thoughts create and shape reality. A lot of these ideas are rooted firmly in hermeticism, occultism, and the mystery religions that most traditions of modern witchcraft point to as their ancestry. However, that can become toxic positivity when we weaponize it against others and ourselves and police very natural human emotions and attitudes in a self-righteous and condescending way.

Positive thinking becomes spiritual bypassing when used as a way to avoid dealing with reality or anything that is uncomfortable. Avoiding reality, our lives, and ourselves isn't the work of the witch, nor is it the teachings of positive thinking in terms of mind over matter. Our negative emotions should be embraced as valuable as they inform us of what we don't want in our lives or ourselves and therefore become a catalyst and motivation for change. Positive thinking is, on the other hand, an unshakable emotional willpower of optimism that acknowledges the current situation, as unsavory as it might be, and intentionally dreams something better into reality. That is a form of magick.

As a Pisces witch, positive thinking is also a form of survival. At times, life can feel insurmountable and we feel completely overwhelmed. In these moments it's important to be the witch who has confidence in their own abilities. It's at these times that our trust in our magick must be unshakeable, even when others doubt us or when immediate changes aren't visible yet. A key to Piscean magick is learning to direct the flow of your thoughts and emotions as subtle energy, without forcing them and drowning in illusion and self-delusion. Dripping water hollows out a stone through persistence and not force. Magickal optimism parallels that for the Pisces witch.

Affirmations for the Pisces Witch

Affirmations are powerful mental tools that can help you reshape the way you think. By repeating positive statements about yourself—worded in the present tense—you can rewire your brain and energy body to create more effective neural pathways and energetic channels within the witch. To make the most of the power of affirmations, you must use them daily and for an extended period of time. With consistent effort, you can unlock the potential of affirmations and achieve great personal growth. Here are some affirmations that may assist you in everyday living as a Pisces witch.

> *I trust in the power of my intuition, psychic ability, and inner wisdom.*
> *I am mindful of when I need to ground and do so.*
> *My imagination is sacred, and I draw power from it.*
> *I am mindful of how much energy I give away.*

A Piscean Blessing of Going Forth

Matthew Venus

In astrological medicine, Pisces is the ruler of our feet. Though we thoroughly rely upon them to travel throughout this world, we tend to take our feet for granted. In this rite, we are honoring and reconnecting with this part of ourselves while calling upon the virtues of Pisces to lend their blessing as we journey along our life's path.

This is a rite that can be performed by anyone to call upon good fortune before we journey, physically or metaphorically, into any new territory. It may be performed before we travel, when beginning a new job or creative project, before an initiation, or whenever we desire to strengthen ourselves and call upon blessings and inspiration as we traverse our daily lives. It may be adapted by those with disabilities for the blessing of the wheels of a wheelchair, feet of canes, and so on. Alter the wording in this rite as feels most appropriate to your needs and desires.

You will need:

+ A large bowl of water
+ A bit of salt, ideally sea salt
+ Pisces oil or olive oil and a bit of lavender oil
+ A clean towel

Instructions:

Choose a bowl or basin that is large enough to comfortably place your foot inside. If this isn't possible, you can always sprinkle our ritual mixture upon your feet instead. Fill the bowl with water of a comfortable temperature.

Take up a bit of the salt in your dominant hand. Cast it into the basin. Stir it into the water in a clockwise direction while saying,

Creature of Water and Creature of Earth.
Water within and without.
Earth within and without.
By sea and by land.
May you be made purified, consecrated, and sanctified.

Next, add a bit of oil to the water. You can use the Pisces oil recipe in this book. Or you could use olive oil to which lavender essential oil has been added or infused with dried lavender buds. Once the oil has been added, hold your hands above the bowl and say,

I call forth and conjure the benevolent spirits of Pisces.
Ruler of the feet.
Beloved of Jupiter and Neptune.
To bless and consecrate this water and oil with your
*   gracious virtues.*
That it may in turn bring blessing to my journeys in
*   this life.*

Use your hands to mix the oil and water together a bit. Take a seat and place the bowl in front of you. You may wish to have the towel down to place your feet upon afterward.

Dip one foot fully into the oil-water mixture, and then the other. You might also like to take a bit of the oil and trace the symbol of Pisces upon each foot with your finger. Massage the mixture into your feet while saying,

> I give gratitude for the blessing of the journey.
> For the path I walk, and the benevolent virtues of Pisces.
> May my intuition safely guide me as I go forth in new terrain.
> May I be led into realms of prosperity, creativity, and opportunity.
> May I be led into realms of personal, spiritual, and magical growth.
> May I stand firm and stable upon the earth and within myself.
> By Pisces, Jupiter, and Neptune may my feet be blessed, may the path be blessed, and good fortune be found wherever my feet may lead.

Dry your feet with the towel. Then go forth into the world with Piscean blessings upon your path.

CONCLUSION

Ivo Dominguez, Jr.

n o doubt, you are putting what you discovered in this book to use in your witchcraft. You may have a desire to learn more about how astrology and witchcraft fit together. One of the best ways to do this is to talk about it with other practitioners. Look for online discussions, and if there is a local metaphysical shop, check to see if they have classes or discussion groups. If you don't find what you need, consider creating a study group. Learning more about your own birth chart is also an excellent next step.

At some point, you may wish to call upon the services of an astrologer to give you a reading that is fine-tuned to your chart. There are services that provide not just charts but full chart readings that are generated by software. These are a decent tool and more economical than a professional astrologer, but they lack the finesse and intuition that only a person can offer. Nonetheless, they can be a good starting point. If you do decide to hire an astrologer to do your chart, shop around to find someone attuned to your spiritual needs. You may decide to learn enough astrology to read your own chart, and that will serve you for many reasons. However, most practitioners of a divinatory art will seek out another practitioner rather than read for themselves in important matters. It is hard to see some things when you are too attached to the outcomes.

If you find your interest in astrology and its effect on a person's relationship to witchcraft has been stimulated by this book, you may wish to read the other books in this series. Additionally, if you have other witches you work with, you'll find that knowing more about how they approach their craft will make your collective efforts more productive. Understanding them better will also help reduce conflicts or misunderstandings. The ending of this book is really the beginning of an adventure. Go for it.

PISCES CORRESPONDENCES

February 19/20–March 20/21

Symbol: ♓

Solar System: Jupiter, Neptune

Season: Winter

Day: Thursday

Celebration: Spring Equinox

Runes: Beorc, Gyfu

Element: Water

Colors: Aqua, Blue (Pale), Green (Light, Sea), Indigo, Lavender, Red, Violet, White, Yellow (Light)

Energy: Yin

Chakras: Brow, Crown

Tarot: Hanged Man, Moon

Trees: Alder, Ash, Cypress, Laurel, Mimosa, Pine, Willow

Herb and Garden: Catnip, Gardenia, Heliotrope, Honeysuckle, Hyacinth, Jasmine. Lavender, Lily, Lovage, Rue, Sage

Miscellaneous Plants: Aloe, Anise, Clove, Nutmeg, Orris Root, Reed, Sandalwood, Star Anise, Water Lily

Gemstones and Minerals: Alexandrite, Amethyst, Aquamarine, Bloodstone, Blue Lace Agate, Cat's Eye, Diamond, Fluorite, Jade, Jasper, Moonstone, Sapphire, Staurolite, Sugilite, Tourmaline (Black), Turquoise

Metal: Silver, Tin

From the Sea: Coral (White), Mother-of-Pearl, Pearl

Goddesses: Aphrodite, Diana, Sedna, Venus

God: Aegir, Cupid, Ea, Enki, Eros, Neptune, Poseidon, Vishnu

Angel: Gabriel

Animals: Cattle (Ox), Horse, Sheep

Birds: Stork, Swan

Marine Life: Seal

Issues, Intentions, and Powers: Adaptability, Calm, Charity, Clarity, Community, Compassion, Creativity, Death, Deceit, Emotions, Enchantment, Endings, Imagination, Intuition, Justice, Kindness, Limitations/Boundaries, Psychic Ability, Romance, Secrets, Sensitivity, Sorrow, Spirituality, Unity

Excerpted with permission from *Llewellyn's Complete Book of Correspondences: A Comprehensive & Cross-Referenced Resource for Pagans & Wiccans* © 2013 by Sandra Kynes.

RESOURCES

Online

Astrodienst: Free birth charts and many resources.

  ✦ https://www.astro.com/horoscope

Astrolabe: Free birth chart and software resources.

  ✦ https://alabe.com

The Astrology Podcast: A weekly podcast hosted by professional astrologer Chris Brennan.

  ✦ https://theastrologypodcast.com

Magazine

The world's most recognized astrology magazine (available in print and digital formats).

  ✦ https://mountainastrologer.com

Books

  ✦ *Practical Astrology for Witches and Pagans* by Ivo Dominguez, Jr.
  ✦ *Parkers' Astrology: The Definitive Guide to Using Astrology in Every Aspect of Your Life* by Julia and Derek Parker

- *The Inner Sky: How to Make Wiser Choices for a More Fulfilling Life* by Steven Forrest
- *Predictive Astrology: Tools to Forecast Your Life and Create Your Brightest Future* by Bernadette Brady
- *Chart Interpretation Handbook: Guidelines for Understanding the Essentials of the Birth Chart* by Stephen Arroyo
- *The Witch's Book of Power* by Devin Hunter

We give thanks and appreciation to all our guest authors who contributed their own special Pisces energy to this project.

H. Byron Ballard

H. Byron Ballard is a WNC native, teacher, and writer. Her books include *Staubs and Ditchwater*, *Asfidity and Mad-Stones*, *Embracing Willendorf*, *Earth Works*, *Roots, Branches and Spirits* and *Seasons of a Magical Life*. She has taught at many festivals and conferences, including Sacred Feminine Rising and the Glastonbury Goddess Festival. She serves as senior priestess at Mother Grove Goddess Temple. Visit her at www.myvillagewitch.com.

Dawn Aurora Hunt

Dawn Aurora Hunt, owner of Cucina Aurora Kitchen Witchery, is the author of *A Kitchen Witch's Guide to Love & Romance* and *Kitchen Witchcraft for Beginners*. Though not born under the sign of Pisces, she combines knowledge of spiritual goals and magickal ingredients to create recipes for all Sun signs in this series. She is a Scorpio. Find her at www .CucinaAurora.com.

Sandra Kynes

Sandra Kynes (Midcoast Maine) is the author of seventeen books, including *Mixing Essential Oils for Magic*, *Magical Symbols and Alphabets*, *Crystal Magic*, *Plant Magic*, and *Sea Magic*. Excerpted content from her book *Llewellyn's Complete Book of Correspondences* has been used throughout this series, and she is a Scorpio. Find her at http://www.kynes.net.

Patricia Lafayllve

Patricia Lafayllve is an author, *gythja*, and *seiðkona* living in Connecticut. She is an Elder in The Troth and has served as Steerswoman, Rede Member, Provost, and High Steward. Patricia is a proud member of Two Ravens Kindred and is active in the Northeast Heathen Community.

Heron Michelle

Heron Michelle (Greenville, NC) is a Modern Hermetic Witch, priestess, and shopkeeper at The Sojourner Whole Earth Provisions (thesojo.com). She is the author of *Elemental Witchcraft: A Guide to Living a Magickal Life Through the Elements* (Llewellyn 2021), blogs at WitchonFire.net, and offers online training. She can be found at HeronMichelle.com.

Thea Sabin

Thea Sabin is the author of *Wicca for Beginners*. At her day job she's an editor and UX writer in EdTech. She comes from a long line of teachers and travelers and has apparently inherited their wanderlust. She lives with a megalomaniacal parrot and loves folklore, ancient history, and bad movies.

Thealandrah

Thealandrah is a priestess drawn to the archetypal energies of the Egyptian pantheon. She has been a member of Light Haven, a contacted mystery school in North Carolina, studying with Aeptha since its inception thirty years ago. Initiated into the Solomonic tradition by Shakmah Winddrum and Aeptha, she is now an adept, Mahceptress, and High Priestess of the lodge.

Matthew Venus

Matthew Venus is a folk magician, artist, and witch. He is the owner of Spiritus Arcanum (IG: @Spiritus_Arcanum, SpiritusArcanum.com), an occult shop focusing on handcrafted incenses and oils, where he also hosts classes and workshops of folk magic, traditional witchcraft, and magical herbalism. He is also the cofounder of the Salem Witchcraft and Folklore Festival. Learn more at www.SalemWitchfest.com.

Notes

Notes

Notes

Notes

Notes

To Write to the Author

If you wish to contact the author or would like more information about this book, please write to the author in care of Llewellyn Worldwide Ltd. and we will forward your request. Both the author and the publisher appreciate hearing from you and learning of your enjoyment of this book and how it has helped you. Llewellyn Worldwide Ltd. cannot guarantee that every letter written to the author can be answered, but all will be forwarded. Please write to:

Ivo Dominguez Jr.
Mat Auryn
℅ Llewellyn Worldwide
2143 Wooddale Drive
Woodbury, MN 55125-2989
Please enclose a self-addressed stamped envelope for reply, or $1.00 to cover costs. If outside the U.S.A., enclose an international postal reply coupon.

Many of Llewellyn's authors have websites with additional information and resources. For more information, please visit our website at:

www.llewellyn.com